MEANING AT WORK

Mary Ann,

I hope you Enjoy
the Journey in the
Book!

MEANING AT WORK

DANNY GUTKNECHT

WITH SUSAN LAHEY

AVIRI PUBLISHING

Published in the United States by Aviri Publishing, Austin, Texas

Library of Congress Cataloging-in-Publication Data
Gutknecht, Danny
    Meaning at Work / Danny Gutknecht – First edition.
Includes biographical references.

ISBN 978-0-9968143-1-7

Printed in the United States of America

Edited by Sarah Beckham
Book Art & Illustrations by Liam Gerrity
Cover Concept by Terence Bennell & Danny Gutknecht
Models: Danny Gutknecht, Bijoy Goswami & Abraham Maslow
Formatting & Aesthetics: Terence Bennell

First Edition

For Melissa, Rachel, Colton.

CONTENTS

FOREWORD

We shall not cease from exploration
And the end of all our exploring
Will be to arrive where we started
And know the place for the first time.

This is one of Danny's favorite quotations and it's a perfect introduction to him and this book. Indeed, his ceaseless explorations have resulted in many a circling back to the start to see with renewed eyes the object of his intense scrutiny. Under his relentless gaze lie two intertwined journeys: that of the individual and the organization. He asks: how do they come together to unleash each other's potential? This book provides the answers he has found thus far.

While your journey will no doubt be enhanced from the insights contained herein, please know that he has a deeper motive in bringing them to you. He'd very much like you to join him as a fellow traveler on his neverending quest. Thus we can confidently quote another famous Briton:

Now this is not the end.
It is not even the beginning of the end.
But it is, perhaps,
the end of the beginning.

Bijoy Goswami
March 2017

Quotes by TS Eliot and Winston Churchill

You can find us on all social media:

@essencemining

Send your thoughts
while reading!

MEANING AT WORK

Listening Experience: **Secret Journey - The Police**

CHAPTER 1

POTENTIAL

Remember when you were a kid, and you took on a project where you worked hard, maybe got sweaty and tired, focused so intensely that when someone called you to dinner, you looked up, shocked? Where had the time gone? You were building a treehouse, souping up your bicycle, creating a restaurant in your backyard. Whatever it was, you were manifesting a vision that completely, utterly, absorbed you. You might have collected small cuts and bruises, wrecked your clothes, forgotten to eat lunch. But all you felt was the exhilaration of bringing your idea to fruition. And while you were deeply engaged, time disappeared.

Imagine if work was like that.

For some people work is like that. It's play. But the vast majority haven't felt like that at work for a long time, maybe ever. They may blame their company, or their boss. And employers, who want employees to be deeply immersed in their work, may try all kinds of new management practices or software to try to address the problem. But solutions elude them both because there's no one-size-fits-all solution to millions of disparate people needing to be inspired, to find meaning, at work. Nonetheless, that's the problem that must be solved.

It's imperative.

MY STORY

When I was 10 years old, I had two passions in life: making money and listening to music. The making money was crucial to listening to music, since I needed a stereo and records. So I took on a paper route, started a lawn-mowing service with two other boys, and ran a tuxedo fish breeding operation to supply the local pet store in Lincoln, Neb. The proceeds went to my music collection.

When I was 14, my uncle Don introduced me to the album *Ghost in the Machine* by The Police. The lyrics intrigued me. The concepts they were singing about seemed to be about something more substantial than most music. A year later I heard Rush's song *"New World Man"* and realized then that it was these songs, songs about creating a better version of yourself, songs that hinted at the possibility of untapped, unexplored potential, that lit a fire inside me. Of course, none of my friends seemed interested in this stuff, so it became a closet hobby for me. Thus began a long, arduous journey of discovering what these things meant.

The older I got, the more obsessed I became with business and music. Only now it was the whole universe of business operations and the profundity of music. Bands like Yes, Tool, and The Police weren't just saying *"Oh baby, baby"* they were communicating concepts like the collective unconscious, synchronicity, anima— the theories of Swiss psychiatrist Carl Jung, who created unique windows into the human experience. College brought a feast in courses like economics, psychology, philosophy, and sociology, but though I wanted to be an entrepreneur, the business courses bored me to tears. Business curriculum in the late '80s focused on how companies like Pepsi, GE, and IBM operated; on macro and microeconomics, statistics, accounting, and law. There was a lot more memorization than insight about strategies and tactics.

Almost none of it was hands-on. So I just took classes I liked, following the thin thread of intuition to see where it took me.

In my third year of college, I started a commercial cleaning company. It was me, my buddy, buckets and brushes, and no idea how to clean anything beyond my apartment and my truck. But thanks to my early experiences, I did know how to sell. In a short time, with a lot of hard work, we had built a sizable company. Washing windows and scrubbing grease off restaurant exhaust hoods gave me lots of time to listen to books on tape on my Walkman. One of these, Tony Robbins' *Awaken the Giant Within*, said he had read something like 700 books. That revelation launched me on a massive reading campaign. Today I'll champion personal experience as the best teacher every time, but it's helpful to have a healthy base of stories and theories on how people grow, achieve success in business and fulfill their potentials.

If I really liked a book, I would look for one that offered a contradictory perspective. It was like entering a warehouse full of ideas about how to make the most of yourself as a human. You're free to wander around, take the ideas apart, build hybrids out of different approaches, and create your own models. The most intriguing got trial tested in my business.

After a few years of growing the cleaning operation, I tried a brief career with a benefits company, running a team that sold health insurance and investment products to small businesses. I've always had a knack for motivating people, and our team was very successful. But the job had only the slightest intersection with the ideas about human and business potential that preoccupied me, so I left.

I wasn't sure what I wanted to do until a Dallas recruiting

company invited me to interview. The offices of this organization were beautiful, the executives dressed to the nines, the training program rigorous. More importantly, the job they did—recruiting doctors to rural locations—looked like a challenge. My gut told me to take the job.

There is a fair amount of complexity in helping physicians sort out career decisions. You need to spend a lot of time listening to both the doctor and hospital to discover how they view the process, and what problems need solving in the hiring interaction. The match can impact both that person's life and the trajectory of the organization, not to mention the lives of patients. Getting these things right became my goal. Ostensibly, the job was selling an opportunity, but I thought that was the wrong approach to such a big decision. The job should be addressing the divide between their hearts and their logic.

I dug in, spending 14 hours a day talking to people about their aspirations and their decision-making processes, what they cared about beyond money, job titles, or the conditioned responses people employ in "job talk." Candidates could sense that I was genuinely curious and not following a script to reach an objective. We quickly dissolved the trivialities and zeroed in on what mattered to them. I was tuning into an essential dialogue. And when you have a dialogue about what is essential, the right things start happening.

The right things started happening for me at the company too. I had been recruiting physicians for only five months when the vice president and CEO asked me to start a new technology-based recruiting business under the corporate umbrella. The first thing out of my mouth was, "I don't know anything about technology." They replied, "We don't either. Just go figure it out."

I had just spent months absorbing the practices, politics,

culture, and rules of recruiting in the medical world and was now doing the same in tech, which at the time was even more foreign than medicine. Most recruiters recommend placements on superficial criteria, a checklist of education and experience. I wanted my employees to understand candidates far more deeply. We recorded every interview to be able to grasp the candidate's skills and function in the organization, as well as what motivated them. All the concepts and models I'd been thinking about since I was 14 found an expansive playground.

Within a few months, we saw that many of the dynamics between the healthcare and technology industries were identical. Whether you were a physician or software developer, competition for highly skilled talent was fierce. Organizations ratcheted up salaries and perks to snag the top candidates, but it wasn't working because these people were already paid well. What organizations weren't addressing was why people did the work they did and how they liked to do it. That was far more important to them than the conversation around money, perks, and status. They had a vision for their careers and their lives, an idea about their potentials. When they perceived that a particular organization could catalyze that vision, they were drawn to it in a way that dollars and benefits couldn't compete with. That's where we wanted recruiters to focus, but it wasn't always easy to persuade them to do so.

Once, a new recruiter approached me full of excitement about a candidate she had just interviewed. She started telling me the candidate's impressive list of credentials. I listened, and replied: "So?"

"So!?" the recruiter responded. "They went to HARVARD!"

"Who cares?" I asked. "Who are they as a person?"

That was the moment it sunk in for her that we were dead

serious that the right person for the job was the one who had a personal connection with the work and the organization, not the candidate with the resume. Yes, skills and experience are important, but passion is what keeps them there. Passion is the fuel that drives their ability to grow, whereas someone with the right credentials but the wrong motivations will probably wind up dialing it in, or worse.

After that, when asked, "Who are they as a person?" the recruiter made sure she had the answer.

Our unique ability to attract and engage some of the best professionals in critical areas created a high demand for our services. But that raised a red flag. Why were so many candidates willing to walk away from jobs where they had relationships, and history, after one conversation about deeper fulfillment? The work world seemed to be full of people whose connections to their jobs were as superficial as the criteria for recruiting them.

Sometimes you know you're unraveling a mystery. Other times, you don't realize it until you've invested a lot of time and energy into tugging on a thread that you just can't let go of. As time progressed, a couple glaring questions crystallized:

- *What is the nature of our connection to work?*
- *How do we create environments that empower people to actualize their potential?*

The prospect of tapping potential en masse in an organization is worthwhile for obvious, and not-so-obvious, reasons. Most of us assume we have more potential than our lives demonstrate. Organizations exist on the idea that they have unrealized potential —growth, expansion, a larger share of the market. But potential, by definition, is something not yet realized. We aren't sure what it will look like, if, and when, it manifests. We don't know what will trigger any person or organization to switch from potential to realization. That's what I wanted to investigate.

WHAT DO PEOPLE WANT?

I've worked with hundreds of companies in industries such as healthcare, technology, finance, and aerospace. I've invested well over 20,000 hours interviewing and collecting data on people in different cultures to find the connection between personal and organizational potential. Here's the key takeaway: We all want to feel that we are truly alive, that our inner, core truth is consistent with the outer reality of our lives. Potential is a big piece of that. So long as our potential is locked up, put away for a future time, our inner truth is inconsistent with our outer reality. There is more to us than we're living. Most of us have moments — a birth or death, getting fired or getting married, a natural disaster or a stellar vacation — when we stop and take stock whether we're living life the way we believe it should be lived. Frequently the answer is lukewarm. Many of us make choices not on the basis of potential, but rather on fear, even if it's just fear of failing convention.

We have become proficient at making money and feeding our outer life at the expense of living a meaningful inner life. In fact, most of the executives and professionals I meet admit this … in confidence. But one doesn't have to come at the expense of the other. Focusing on meaning and work can make both better.

Today we still seem to cling to the paradigm that employment is an exchange of time for dollars. Employees see employers as a means to provide the money for what they need and want; employers see employees as bundles of talents, skills, and potential that can be quantified and channeled toward profit. We rarely address the innate need to do work that we believe is meaningful, that brings us alive. This is because we have highly developed tools for measuring things like science and commerce, but our tools for understanding meaning and human potential are much less precise. Because we don't have the right tools, we use the wrong ones—tools that standardize the one thing you can't standardize: people.

STANDARD HUMANS, STANDARD COMPANIES

Procrustes was the blacksmith son of Poseidon who stopped passers-by on the sacred path between Athens and Eleusis, inviting them to stay the night. Once he got them inside, he insisted that they be "fitted" to his iron bed. If they were too large to fit the bed, he lopped off body parts. If they were too small, he stretched them. His reign of terror finally ended when he was captured and decapitated to fit the bed. Hence the expression *Procrustean bed*, an arbitrary standard to which exact conformity is forced.

Too many organizations function as Procrustean beds. They want people with specific skills and experience who fit neatly into their preformatted culture. They think it makes managing people easier if they all fit the dimensions. But no one exactly fits their paradigm. So they "lop off" the bits that don't conform— personality traits, interests, passions that don't align with the culture. They stretch people, expecting them to wholeheartedly embrace a system that doesn't resonate with them.

And today, employees are responding in kind, saying, "This organization doesn't fit," "That organization doesn't fit" and leaving a costly wake of disengagement, expensive turnover costs, cultural decimation, and a steady leak of institutional knowledge. But as Jung pointed out, there is no such thing as a standard person. And most of the ways we try to quantify culture fit leave out more of who the person is than they include.

The big tool most companies use to find out who their employees are and what they want are surveys. Surveys can be useful, but also dangerous. Such tests reduce people to cartoon figures, two-dimensional versions of themselves that give you a two-dimensional perspective on your culture and potential.

Jung noted that psychological tests—and the same applies for surveys—only measure a small number of factors in a group of people, resulting in a mean and a median. The world then takes this mean or median to be "normal," and people determine they should adjust themselves so that they more closely resemble that "norm." But he said that was like measuring a riverbed full of pebbles and discovering that the average weight was 145 grams. You might then say that a "normal" pebble weighed 145 grams. But if you looked all day, you might never actually find a single pebble that weighed exactly 145 grams.[1]

In fact, in pronouncing pebbles as having an average weight of 145 grams you would be in danger of thinking you knew a lot about them, while still having no idea where they came from or how they arrived here, what kind of rock they were or how they'd been altered through their journey. You wouldn't know about their color or shape variations, whether some were geodes, bore fossils, or wore the scars of some historic cataclysm.

Jung noted that all the ways of measuring humans that define a mean, or average, of some set of attributes leave out dozens of other attributes, so the results are only valuable in a really narrow set of circumstances. Organizations function in this way. In creating a job description for a new hire, they define a narrow set of attributes valuable to a particular position, team, or organization, and hold candidates or employees up against that model. Like in Jung's psychological tests, we treat attributes that don't fit in our paradigm as "outliers" to be ignored or viewed with concern.

But these very attributes, the things that make us unique, are the source of breakthroughs, creativity, and innovation.

Michael Porter, a seminal thinker whose work serves as gospel for many top management consulting firms, points out in his book *On Competition* that treating business as a competition with one winner is often a flawed strategy. Porter claims that businesses can coexist and thrive when each focuses on its unique value.[2]

Uniqueness, however, is seen as anathema to efficiency, so organizations mute it, resulting in cultures that reward homogeneity. This fails to account for the reality that companies are culturally and generationally diverse. Aiming for standardization and scale may seem to make it easier to manage people, but it makes you more vulnerable to competition based on price or value. More importantly it becomes more difficult for employees, and eventually customers, to make an essential connection to the organization.

Just as it is for individuals, tapping your uniqueness as an organization is critical to tapping your potential. Companies know this, but often, like individuals, feel chained by the very processes that feed them.

We need tools and models that meet the demands of business today, accounting for unique contribution without disrupting the current value chain. Current methods used to increase motivation tend to oversimplify how people work, and thus become counterproductive. It is clear that we spend too much time chasing *"The Five Keys to Success," "The Three Things Every*

Worker Wants," or other management flavors of the month. These are pointless exercises that reduce people to formulas and draw the cognitive power away from the real conversations that need to happen.

What is at stake goes beyond reaching a different level of engagement, innovation, and performance to the organization. It has implications for humanity. Envision a world where most people wake up excited about the problems they will solve and the contribution they will make at work that day. They're excited about the coworkers with whom they share a sense of mission that transcends racial, cultural, and generational barriers. They measure the value of their days by the experience of feeling fully alive.

Making this a reality is complex in that it must be done in a way that actually works with how humans process meaning. If there is one thing the "user experience" movement has taught us, it's that humans have their own, natural and instinctive way of functioning. Efforts to retrain us often fail, and many of us will break or abandon systems set up to manage our behavior. We are meaning creatures from the day we're born and we already have internal systems for processing meaning. So organizations can't just supply meaning. Nor can you reduce it to identifying types of work that are generally considered meaningful. Context matters.

I once had a client, a healthcare organization, that had just invested $1 million hiring a superstar physician and setting up a brand-new clinic and service line for the system. They wanted me to spend time with him and his staff so we could define a recruiting message to help build his practice. After I interviewed the physician, my client asked, "What did you think? He's great isn't he?"

I agreed. "He is great. But this whole investment is in trouble. You might want to start looking for a backup plan to replace him."

My client looked at me with disbelief. "Why do you say that? He graduated from one of the best programs in the country. He loves the location."

"Yeah, I know," I said. "He's a great guy, probably a great doctor, and he likes this organization. But who he is, and how he wants to work, are different from who this organization is and how it does things." What the physician found meaningful and what the organization found meaningful didn't resonate. They both were heading in good directions, but they weren't the same direction.

Sure enough, nine months later, the doctor left. Neither the doctor nor the organization had anything but the best intentions. The relationship worked on paper, in form and function, but the essence of who each was, and what was meaningful to them, was not aligned. It is remarkable how many professional relationships and organizations are blocked from their full potential by this fundamental lack of alignment. This hinders our progress economically, scientifically, and politically.

Today, organizations, employees, and business thought leaders are beginning to discuss the role of meaning at work more openly and urgently. In response to this overwhelming workforce trend, companies are beginning to redefine management practices, HR, and organizational development. Large organizations have the biggest challenge because of their sheer numbers. Many have tried to solve the problem by copying other successful cultures – often with disastrous results. The elements that create "magic" in one company fit another like a bad suit.

The hard truth is organizations can't give people meaning. They can try—and it might work temporarily. But that's not the function of an organization. In fact, the evangelism of corporate values often creates the very problem it is trying to solve, by inspiring a mechanical adherence to values that may be on the wall, but not in an employee's own makeup. Nor can the company live up to those values.

And for some companies meaning is lip service. They say they care, but they have no intention of creating a great place to work beyond quarter-to-quarter results.

Great companies do care about this. They understand the complexity of issues at play: the importance of a mission that runs through the organization's veins, the factors necessary for engagement and creativity, the danger of being easily replicated. They know they can't sit on their laurels on old organizational models or fix their problems with off-the-shelf management solutions. They have to understand their people and their business deeply, and become a place where their employees can make a difference for the company, while also spending time in work that makes them feel truly alive.

This book explains how.

Listening Experience: **Money Shot - Puscifer**

CHAPTER 2

THE DISCONNECT

You've read the statistics.

In the U.S., only one in three employees is engaged, defined by Gallup as involved in, enthusiastic about, and committed to their work. So if you run a company, it's likely that two out of three people you're paying to work for you are barely dialing it in. Globally it's worse, only 13 percent of people are engaged.[3] It doesn't matter whether you're talking to a doctor or a supply chain manager, whether they're male or female, in Denver or Dubai. It's global discontent.

About 20 percent of employees are what Gallup calls "actively disengaged." These individuals are working against your organization because they're "busy acting out their unhappiness." A merely disengaged employee is one who is doing the bare minimum within set expectations, not putting any extra effort or creativity into the work. Actively disengaged employees spend their time on social media or looking for jobs during work time, while undermining managers and sowing discontent among peers. Gallup estimated in 2013 that actively disengaged people cost the U.S. economy up to $550 billion in lost productivity every year.[4] Curt Coffman, global practice leader for Q12 Management Consulting and coauthor of Gallup's management book First,

Break All the Rules, dubbed these workers CAVE dwellers: Consistently Against Virtually Everything. Their behavior sabotages the effort and momentum built by other people in your organization.

Coffman's CAVE Dwellers reminded me of Plato's allegory of the cave: It's the story of people who have spent their lives chained in a cave, forced to look only in one direction, watching shadows thrown against the wall by people moving outside the cave. They have no idea that there's another world, or that the shadows are only shadows. Plato points out that anyone who broke out of the cave would struggle, at first, to ascertain which was reality—the cave world, or the world outside. But having adjusted to sunlight, air, and humans, they would likely be inspired to return to the cave to free those still chained. To their disappointment, the cave dwellers would probably treat their glad tidings with hostility, condemning any description of a different realm as delusional and even dangerous.

Plato was talking about intellectual enlightenment. But the allegory fits as well to describe Coffman's CAVE dwellers, who have resigned themselves to the idea that they must work to survive, and for whom a description of work as something transcendent must feel like a mockery. Asking them to get excited about it is expecting something they can't even conceptualize. For that reason, they will undermine any possibility that there may be something better.

The people who escape the cave and discover the world outside are the minority who are deeply, personally invested in the work and how it gets done. They get fired up working with others who share their enthusiasm and focus. This group can include anyone from leaders to frontline employees who are motivated to make a contribution that matters—both to the organization and to everyone the organization serves. They are responsible and empowered. From the CAVE dweller's perspective, they're speaking gibberish.

The next figure, the 50 percent that Gallup calls passively disengaged, aren't entirely checked out, but their heart isn't in it. They understand the idea of being passionate about their work and may even experience it from time to time. But it totally depends on circumstances—the right team, the right project, the right client. Disengaged employees know that some people show up every day inspired and feel fulfilled in their work and lives. They'd love to have that experience, but can't imagine where to start. You'll often hear a disengaged employee call someone who loves their work "lucky."

These statistics paint a picture of a road to nowhere populated by disgruntled, disinterested employees. But while the statistics capture the prevailing attitudes in the workplace, they don't explain why. In my experience, most employees want to be enthusiastic about their jobs. They launch into a new job hoping it will be a conduit toward what they consider a better life. When they invest time and effort at work, they believe it is going toward that better future. But over time, many discover that the vision in their heads doesn't align with the reality. There's no connection between what the company says it's about and the tasks they have to perform.

Switching jobs takes time and energy. After a few experiences of getting excited about a job that seems to morph once they're in it, many people are discouraged. It seems easier to accept that employment is a prosaic necessity that pays the bills, rather than repeat this challenging ritual, looking for something that doesn't appear to be available to them.

The disengaged employees' malaise is all the more painful to them because our culture often touts passionate commitment to one's work as a hallmark of a good life.

So the narrative that begins to play out is "What's wrong with me? Where did the spark go?" "Why can't I find a job I care about?" Or conversely, "They sold me a bill of goods about this company" or "I would be happy if it weren't for my manager, etc. ..." Even if you're in a hot industry, the prospect of personal growth is always present and often just around the next bend. The cognitive discomfort is what compels people to disengage.

Researcher William Kahn talks about the relationship between individuals and the roles they play at work. The more closely aligned the individual is with what is expected in the role, the more satisfied they'll be. But there's often a huge disconnect between the individual's idea of themselves in the role, and what the organization expects. As they're learning to fit into the culture, they begin to see how the role is viewed differently by others in the organization and that their performance will be judged by others. So their own idea of the role gets lost. Kahn wrote:

> *In engagement, people employ and express themselves physically, cognitively, and emotionally during role performances [...] personal disengagement [is] the uncoupling of selves from work roles; in disengagement, people withdraw and defend themselves physically, cognitively, or emotionally during role performances.*[5]

This is life in the "safe zone," at the bottom of the foxhole. You can hear it in the things people say at work. "I don't know why we do it this way..." "I would take action, but we..."

Employees have come to see the culture, the hierarchy, or

the politics as insurmountable obstacles that keep them shackled to prescribed actions. So the work that they do feels meaningless, the antithesis of a life well lived. Employees drift from job to job looking for meaning or give up on trying to find it and just put in the bare minimum.

But no one finds deep satisfaction living that way. So what is deeply satisfying work?

DEEPLY SATISFYING WORK

A sense of wider meaning to one's existence is what raises a man beyond mere getting and spending. If he lacks this sense, he is lost and miserable. —**Carl Jung**

The only happy people I know are the ones who are working well at something they consider important ... This was a universal truth for all my self-actualizing subjects. —**Abraham Maslow**

The person who takes a job in order to live—that is to say, for the money—has turned himself into a slave. —**Joseph Campbell**

Most people know of American psychologist Abraham Maslow's Hierarchy of Needs, generally represented as a layered triangle with food, shelter, and safety at the bottom and self-actualization at the top. But fewer are familiar with his prolific writings, what self-actualization really means, or that he was working on a revised theory toward the end of his life. Maslow's theory mapped human motivation to the pursuit of a progressive evolution of needs he believed were essential for a healthy existence. For example, our physical needs for food and safety may motivate us to seek a job, but once those needs are satisfied, another critical need emerges, like the need for belonging or love.

31

Once all the other needs are met, we realize that we still have one need left: the need to fulfill our potentials. Maslow called this point of personal evolution *self-actualization*. Before self-actualization, people often use work to shore up an identity through money, status, belonging—things they must get from other people. Self-actualizing people have gotten to a place where they see that such things have limited value. Instead, they focus not on how their peers see them, but on what they can produce or create that they consider worth pursuing. For self-actualizing people, work is play. They enjoy the opportunity to test themselves and grow, to produce something better today than was there yesterday. They focus on the work itself.

Maslow began to revise his theory toward the end of his life. He noted that while the self-actualizers he studied were healthy people, there was another type of person who was not only healthy but who seemed to tap into the magic and beauty of life in a way that helped them transcend a lot of the mundane behaviors of others:

> Perhaps we could say that the description of the healthy ones is … primarily as strong identities, people who know who they are, where they are going, what they want, what they are good for, in a word, as, strong Selves, using themselves well and authentically and in accordance with their own true nature.
>
> And this, of course, does not sufficiently describe the transcenders. They are … this; but they are also more than this.[6]

He called these transcenders "Peakers." They are people for whom peak experiences are the most important value. A peak experience doesn't have to be the birth of a child or climbing Mount Everest. It can be just a moment when you are disconnected from time and space in that you are completely and positively absorbed by something. Mihaly Csikszentmihalyi's "flow" state—being "in the zone" with your work—could be called a peak experience. Some people, Maslow pointed out, value this experience over safety or belonging. Maslow said Peakers operate from values like "aliveness." A Peaker would be more likely to seek out jobs where peak experiences are likely:

> *They are more likely to be innovative, creators of the new because they can see what exists in potentia—and therefore what might be brought to pass.[7]*

While Maslow observed exemplars, people who had accomplished great things, and then re-engineered their psychology to see how they became so, Jung studied the path of becoming personally whole through a process he called *individuation*. Both were focusing on people they found to be uniquely comfortable with themselves, who seemed to live in a way that was transcendent of the norms. These people had a realistic perspective on themselves, they knew their flaws and their humanity, but they still reached unabashedly for their higher potentials. An individuated person integrates both the conscious parts of the self—the parts people generally want to present—and the unconscious, often hidden parts of the self that Jung called "the shadow." The conscious parts of the self seek external validation, external rewards, acceptance by others. What dwells in the unconscious, however, is often the parts that make us unique, creative, surprising.

Another person who examined the rarely traveled path to manifesting potential is Joseph Campbell, author of *The Power of Myth*. Campbell said we all have an inner calling to forgo comfort and take what he calls a Hero's Journey. The Hero's Journey demands we test the limits of what we know we can do and find it within ourselves to become more. But this journey is always preceded by a period of doubt, hesitation, and struggle. Like Plato's cave dwellers, we fear to leave the comforts of familiar, external truths to the unknown territory that is our unconscious.

Throughout history, scholars, artists, scientists, and business people have pointed to what appears to be a human calling to transcend our perceived limits so that we can contribute something unique and meaningful. To let our outer actions—in many cases our work—express what is important to the compelling drives of our human souls.

Those same thinkers have expressed the sense of emptiness that comes when people feel that calling is thwarted. Everyone studying and researching the human condition recognizes that there is something inside that yearns for more: Meaning, meaningful contribution, a need to fully embrace and manifest one's unique identity. Even if it is a contribution to a team effort, people hunger to be able to say. "I was here, and it mattered." This isn't a statement about computer programmers or sales executives or teachers. It's a statement about people. Regardless of our job title, our industry, this is how humans are. Some people recognize this in themselves and seek opportunities to manifest it. Others may not reflect this principle at all, but in my experience, that's often because they simply don't know such a thing is possible for them. They don't know how to translate their thoughts about fulfillment and their ideas about work into a language that would serve both. And some fear such a connection isn't possible. So it's easier to discount or repress personal calling.

Can organizations solve this for employees? Not in the

sense of providing meaning. But Maslow, Jung and Campbell recognized that the culture itself—whether organizational or social—is monumentally important to the actualization and activation of individual potentials. Leaders are well aware of some tactics that can inspire people to work toward their potential: transparency, flatter hierarchies, supportive management. But there are even more specific tactics for helping employees draw the connections between what they find meaningful and the work they've chosen to do. There are ways to make the synergy between the individual and the role much easier and more fulfilling and enduring. Organizations are in a unique position to grow and profit by unleashing this fundamental human drive.

Creating an organization that performs for the customer depends on everyone in the organization taking personal responsibility to continuously develop deep levels of expertise. Organizations need employees who are attentive to the small, iterative change that delivers value—not sleepwalking through their jobs. If you want to tap this kind of potential in your company, you need to understand not only how humans are motivated, but how to empower individual self-development, at scale.

Before we examine how to do that, let's look at how we got where we are today.

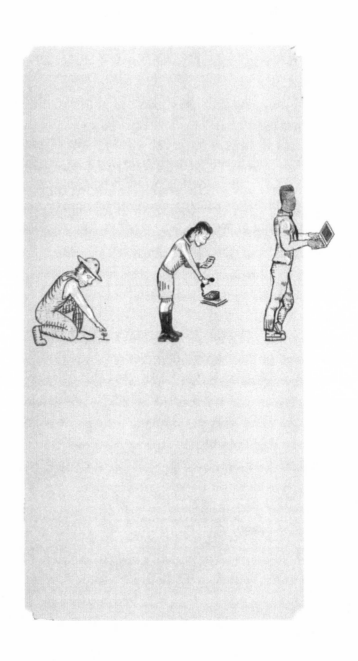

Listening Experience: **Stinkfist - Tool**

CHAPTER 3

NEEDLES THAT MAKE A HAYSTACK

If you think about the way we've addressed motivating employees to perform, it maps—in many ways—with the tiers of Maslow's hierarchy. Work was rewarded with pay, which employers assumed would be enough—it supplied food and safety needs. But as it turned out, once that need was met, other needs arose: the need to feel esteem, to have a connection with coworkers, and today, the need for self-actualization. The research on motivation that's been going on for 100 years has revealed a lot about our relationship to work.

During the transition from an agrarian to an industrial society, most workers grabbed whatever jobs they could. They just wanted to secure for themselves and their families enough money to survive—to get a roof over their heads and food to eat. In turn, most employers assumed that pay was all they needed to motivate employees.

But then came a growing interest in the science and technology of efficiency, spawning decades of research into how to treat people in order to increase production and profits.

In 1909, Frederick Taylor published *The Principles of Scientific Management*. Taylor was an engineer who was fascinated by efficiency. He believed that the biggest waste in organizations was not materials but human effort. (Yes, we had effort problems in the 1900s.) His studies showed him that certain people could work more efficiently than others. He suggested those people should be targeted for hiring. He also developed ideas that shape our workplaces even today:

- *Pay should be tied to performance.*
- *Workers should be matched to their jobs based on capability and motivation rather than just attaching the first warm body to the first empty machine or task.*
- *Managers should take a mentor-like, supervisory role with workers, (rather than ignoring them as they had before).*

At the time Taylor was doing his research, manufacturing employees were compensated for the number of units or pieces produced. Employers literally reduced the amount per piece for the most productive workers so that they wouldn't make too much money. Clearly, this wasn't very motivating! Taylor convinced factory owners that they could make more money by paying the most productive employees more. This gave employees more control over their success, a great motivator. With the new emphasis on promoting people who showed initiative, workers had more of a chance to be chosen as a manager, or switched to a more suitable job, based on their skills and efforts.

With the changes Taylor inspired, employees could not only meet their survival needs at work, but they could also fulfill some of their esteem needs. They were moving up Maslow's model.

At the same time Taylor was doing his research, Max Weber and Frank and Lillian Gilbreth were also forming theories that influence how we work to this day. They believed there was one right way to do things, and that a hierarchy of authority and command, with clearly defined responsibilities, was the best way to foster efficiency and productivity. These are some of the very doctrines that, now ingrained in our organizational psyches, bog down our ability to innovate.

THE POWER OF RELATIONSHIPS

In the 1920s and 1930s, Elton Mayo, an Australian-born sociologist, led the Hawthorne Studies. In these studies, employees at Western Electric's factory in the Chicago suburb of Hawthorne were subjected to a number of changes—like different light levels, working hours, and rest breaks—to gauge their effect on workers' productivity.

The results were puzzling. When the researchers increased the lighting for one group, productivity increased. On the other hand, when they decreased the lighting, productivity tended to go up, too. After doing these experiments over 12 years, Mayo and others eventually concluded that the changes themselves didn't prompt increases or decreases in productivity. What boosted productivity was simply that employees felt they were treated like people. The fact that someone cared about their well-being enough to address something as simple as lighting raised productivity.

In addition, Mayo realized that people who worked in groups benefited enormously from that camaraderie. The efficiency produced by Taylor had separated individuals. Employees were happier in teams and developed their own social contracts around who was a good leader or teammate. This was an early appearance of what would later be called the Informal Organization or the Black Box, which holds enormous power over organizational culture. Mayo's research helped promote the idea that people who had their social needs met at work experienced a sense of belonging—the third tier in Maslow's hierarchy.

In the process of interviewing 21,000 workers, he realized that people needed to talk, in a freeform way, about the deep emotional connection between their lives and their work. They would begin talking about work, but often go into stories about their families and other aspects of their lives. Mayo believed the industrial revolution had destroyed the bonds that had existed among those in the skilled trades of the 19th century and workers were trying to rebuild them. As one writer paraphrased Mayo:

> *The social cohesion holding democracy together ... was predicated on these collective relationships, and employees' belief in a sense of common purpose and value of their work.*[8]

That hasn't changed.

THE DRUCKER REVOLUTION

In recognizing the idea of people's individual, value-driven connection to their work, Mayo ushered in the behavioral science school of management, which factored in people's values, motivations, and personalities. The leading luminary of the period was Peter Drucker, who published *The Practice of Management* in 1954. This book revolutionized our ideas about how people should operate within a company. Drucker was called "The Man Who Invented Management." He introduced the concept of Management by Objectives, or Management by Results, suggesting that employees would be better motivated if they understood the company's targets and could help set goals, rather than just being given a task. He coined the term "knowledge workers" in 1959, laying the groundwork for the shift from "human resources" to "talent."

Drucker realized that we were moving into a knowledge economy, but that all of our methods of employee motivation were based on studies of factory workers: production, not performance. We needed a different approach for the new type of workplace. Inviting people to give their input and take ownership in the company's success exponentially raises the level of belonging and esteem over merely doing a task well. It also creates a culture that empowers more individual development and uniqueness because it lets employees help define organizational values and identity.

WHAT REALLY MOTIVATES

Frederick Herzberg introduced a theory of employee motivation in 1959 based on a study of how motivators—including money, autonomy, and mastery—affected performance. It concluded that more money does not motivate people when they are doing work that involves cognitive skills. In fact, too much money can de-motivate.

Herzberg identified two sets of factors that impacted motivation. Hygiene Factors included security, salary, fringe benefits, and work conditions. These weren't motivators, Herzberg said, but their absence de-motivated employees. They take care of the lower rungs of Maslow's hierarchy. But to motivate behavior you need to offer something else. Herzberg's Motivators included challenging work, recognition, and responsibility—the same types of motivators Peter Drucker was onto. These correspond with the needs Maslow identified about halfway up his hierarchy.

In the 1980s, a theory of motivation that Edward Deci and others had been working on for more than a decade finally gained acceptance as scientifically valid. Self-Determination Theory states that there are both extrinsic motivators—praise, recognition, money—and intrinsic motivators—autonomy, competence, relatedness. Relatedness, the need to do something that shows care for others, was a significant breakthrough in motivation research. Others had already proven that competence or mastery and autonomy were important motivators. But they hadn't focused on the idea that people would work better if they were working to help others. Organizations have made efforts to incorporate these kinds of motivators in recent years.

You may be familiar with a 2005 motivation study done by the Boston Federal Reserve Bank and made famous by Daniel Pink. This study addressed a workforce that was significantly different from the one of just two decades before. When a cognitive skill is involved in work, it said, some of the chief motivators include the ability of employees to do things their own way, and to become masters at their skill sets. This is the kind of stuff that motivates people who want to contribute something unique through their work.

NEXT-LEVEL MOTIVATION

Organizations can draw on all of this research to spur better performance, increase profits, and gain a competitive edge. And the data are very clear here: Organizations with engaged, productive workforces outperform organizations with unmotivated workforces by more than 300 percent.[9]

Most companies have become relatively adept at identifying and promoting top employees to management. They have systems that reward efficiency and productivity. They involve employees in goal setting, and they foster some level of workplace camaraderie.

So why does engagement remain low? Why are we still struggling to get large numbers of employees to invest their hearts and minds in their work?

This is where motivation gets complicated. Good pay, solid

colleagues, trust from managers, and an enjoyable environment can all make employees happier. They might contribute to performance. Having a stake in the outcome can inspire commitment. Many top-performing organizations have done a good job of these things.

EVOLUTION OF SOCIETAL FOUNDATIONS

But we're in a different ballgame now. To compete, organizations must inspire people to get invested in what they're doing and make the best choices for the organization and the customer. Constant innovation demands employees who pay attention to market and audience shifts and offer creative solutions. As Uber disrupted the taxi industry and Airbnb disrupted the hotel industry, every organization needs people who are sensitive to the cultural shifts that signal it's time to iterate. Companies perceived as innovative have much higher brand loyalty. Companies that innovate ahead of the curve, based on changes in consumer behavior, establish their value in the market.

Some organizations have concluded that all such iterations are the actions of "stars" and that the rock star or ninja employee is the panacea to performance and engagement problems. After all, stars are already motivated. They're already creative. All we need to do is get more of them on the payroll to inspire everyone else to up their game. But that's a crapshoot. What motivates someone to take a job doesn't necessarily motivate that person to perform six months down the road. Nor does it motivate the star to stay at the company when a higher bidder comes along. Moreover, what drives someone to star behavior in one context doesn't translate to all other contexts. It's the chemistry between the employee and the culture of the organization. It's not about incentivizing classes of people to do things; it's about making sure individuals have the opportunity and encouragement to contribute something unique to something that already matters to them.

A more appropriate model for today may be Peter Senge's Learning Organization, which demands that everyone strive for the level of personal introspection, responsibility, and ownership that self-actualizing people tend to exhibit. But what do we do with the organizations we have, today, to get them where they need to be? It doesn't take a rocket scientist to see that traditional concepts of management are quickly losing effectiveness to the point of being irrelevant, as today's business environment calls upon workers to understand themselves, their work, and the world around them at higher levels of complexity.

The actively disengaged may never decide to find a solution

to their discontent. But as for the 50 percent who are merely disengaged, dialing it in, the question is: What could inspire them to dig in, engage, perform? What could motivate them to focus on making the product, service, and experience better for customers and for their fellow workers? How can organizations help tie the fulfillment of individual potential to the realization of organizational potential?

Maslow and Jung both concluded that personal meaning fuels human potential. Harvard professor Teresa Amabile, a psychologist and workplace motivation expert who wrote *The Progress Principle*, did research that confirmed their assertion. Amabile conducted lengthy investigations into the inner lives and performance of teams. She and her partner, Steven Kramer, collected 12,000 diary entries from professionals writing about their daily experiences at work. Their research showed that people in knowledge-based industries perform when they're making progress in meaningful work. And, as the researchers stated in an HBR article, for the Progress Principle to operate, the work must be meaningful to the person doing it.[10]

Employees must be able to see the connection between what they find meaningful and the work they do for the organization. There's usually a connection; people end up in jobs for a reason. But it's incumbent on organizations to create environments that help employees make the connection. The success of the organization and of the individual both depend on it. Lack of engagement is the symptom, not the disease.

The way to a thriving, growing, creative workforce is through the door of meaning.

Listening Experience: **Prime Mover - Rush**

CHAPTER 4

MEANING THROUGH THE LOOKING GLASS

Lewis Carroll's book *Through The Looking-Glass and What Alice Found There* explores the underlying rules that govern our existence. It examines the process of growing up as a struggle to comprehend these rules, but also questions where these rules come from and the nature of reality. What is meaning and who is in charge of it?

People have been battling over meaning since the dawn of time. Religions, political systems, philosophies have all formed to give people an explanation regarding the meaning of their lives. People have been sacrificed for it, gone to war over it, made pilgrimages, and taken hallucinogens to find it. The variety of ways people have sought meaning, and the things they've lost in pursuit of it, is mind-boggling.

While each of us can identify something we believe is meaningful, meaning itself has been difficult to pin down. It's different from one culture to another, one neighborhood or family or person to another. It also changes over our lives, through our experiences.

In other words, meaning is a powerful driver for human development and identity, but it's also amorphous, multifarious, and personal. How does an organization incorporate something like that into its business model?

The Academy of Management, an organization dedicated to the advancement of management and administration, hosted a conference whose theme was "Making Organizations Meaningful." So I attended. The conference participants were mostly PhDs and included academics from institutions like Oxford, Wharton, Harvard, and Hohenheim. This is only one of many conferences held in recent years on this topic. The amount of intellectual energy being devoted to it shows it can no longer be ignored. It's gone from "soft stuff" in the organization to "We need to figure this out."

Most organizations have only begun exploring this idea. And because the way meaning works is not well understood, they're using the wrong tools, trying to provide blanket solutions to address a host of individual disconnects. They are relying on company values, creating volunteer opportunities, donating a portion of profits to charity. All those things can make employees feel better about their employers, but they can't make the work itself personally meaningful. If the point is for people to plug into work and get fulfillment from it, such broad cultural gestures won't work.

I DON'T WANT TO BUILD A CATHEDRAL

Because we don't understand meaning, we tend to oversimplify it. We think of some ideas and actions as belonging in the "meaning bucket" while others don't. Being a doctor, for example, is meaningful; making widgets isn't. But that's nonsense. Depending on the widget and the worker, making widgets could be more meaningful in some cases.

It's easy to resort to this kind of simplistic thinking to address the meaning question. We build companies to provide goods and services and in the process have to wrestle with market challenges, economic shifts, and regulations. Though almost every company has to deal with meaning, meaning isn't seen as a core business issue. So companies find efficient ways to weave meaning in. One method is to attach a "meaningful" idea to the product or company in the hope of engendering an emotional connection among employees and customers. For example, Coca-Cola CMO Marcos de Quinto once attested: "We make simple everyday moments more special."[11] That's a lot more meaningful than "We make carbonated sugar water." But does that idea actually viscerally inspire the people who mix and bottle Coke, the QA engineers, and the people who stock the convenience store fridges? Does it satisfy their need to contribute to what they believe matters?

A classic example of this effort to create an overarching 'meaning' is the story of the three bricklayers, often told by managers and organizational leaders to spark employees' enthusiasm. In the story, someone asks three bricklayers what they're doing. One says they're earning $20 an hour. Another says they're putting one brick on top of the other. The third says they're building a cathedral, a house for God. According to the standard version of this story, Bricklayer No. 3 wins the meaning contest by finding something profound about the job.

But unless those three bricklayers were blank slates before they got there — which none of your employees are — it's a mistake to assume they're all going to get jazzed about building a cathedral. Let's say the person who says they're putting one brick on top of another isn't expressing futility, but a life philosophy that great things are built by focusing on doing each small step correctly. Maybe the person earning $20 an hour grew up in poverty and the money signifies their children won't have to endure the deprivation they did. Bricklayers No. 1 and 2 may be less concerned with what the building will eventually be than they are with how their work feeds what they believe is meaningful. Everyone in your organization has a story about why they're there. If you assume it's all roughly the same story, or that unless they're all building cathedrals, they aren't connected to something bigger, you're not seeing things as they are. Such thinking reduces a complex culture into an overly simplistic artifact. This almost always limits individual potential en masse. It's Procrustes all over again.

Whole Foods founder John Mackey recognized the need for a meaningful connection with work and was an early pioneer to tackle the meaning problem. He even recognized the importance of having employees contribute to the mission à la Peter Drucker. Whole Foods is guided by a list of aspirations, including providing customers with healthy food and revealing that food's environmental and social footprint.[12] Mackey invited 60 people, early in the company's history, to draft Whole Foods' Declaration of Interdependence, which essentially defines their culture. In a sense, they had a chance to define Whole Foods' meaning at that point in time.

But it hasn't been revised in 20 years, making it an artifact of a culture created by people who may not even work there anymore. It probably does inspire new employees, even though they had no hand in drafting it. But it's unlikely to inspire them in the same way it engaged those who were responsible for putting their own thought into it. When an organization has a static meaning model, employees can either get behind it, leave, or stay and do their work for the social and financial rewards. It's my experience that a lot of employees take the last course. Offering good pay and benefits, along with a good cause, can encourage good work initially. But it can't tap individual potential in the same way as having that sense of ownership for what the organization becomes.

Sometimes organizations try to bolster engagement by making wholesale changes to the organizational meaning by importing something that might seem sexier or more 'en vogue.' In 2011, JCPenney hired former Apple retail chief Ron Johnson as CEO to remake the JCPenney customer experience, Apple-style. The experiment failed, to the tune of a 25 percent sales drop, an operating loss of nearly $1 billion, and a public skewering of Johnson himself. Rather than praise his efforts to make JCPenney cool, experts and pundits questioned why Johnson was hired when he so obviously hated the company brand.[13] The culture must be authentic to who you are to have a positive impact, especially among those who are there because of who you are.

THE EMPLOYEES WHO KNOW WHO YOU ARE

I worked with an engineering firm that had just scored a contract designing multiple iterations of a product within a strict regulatory environment. They needed to hire a lot of great engineers very quickly. The general manager knew that many engineers love working on projects with full life cycle development, where they get to design things, then see them being created on the factory floor—where they can touch them all the way through. This project offered full life cycle development, so that's how the manager drew candidates to the job. Many highly skilled engineers came to work on the project. And many fled almost as soon as they had started. The turnover was killing their ability to deliver, and their reputation was being damaged, so they brought us in.

We interviewed engineers who had left and those who had stayed. We discovered that those who left did so because the job was demanding, the hours were long, the task seemed impossible, and they never tackled the same problem twice.

As it turned out those who stayed did so for the exact same reasons. They loved being the Navy SEALS of the engineering world. They kept saying, "Not everyone can handle this job," and "Every day we're dealing with something we've never dealt with before." One engineer said: "It's like being dropped in the middle of the ocean with no shore in sight, so you start swimming. But when you finally find the beach, it's a fantastic beach." The situation was pushing them to discover and fulfill their potentials.

So the company began selling the job as an opportunity for those who wanted a tough challenge, and it worked. The right people came, ready to dig in and prove themselves. The general manager's mistake—a common one in organizations—was to decide what was meaningful about the work, rather than asking employees what they were about and what they found meaningful.

Meaning at work isn't just the latest feel-good management fad. It significantly impacts organizational success. Dan Ariely, professor of behavioral economics at Duke University, has done a number of studies and experiments gauging the importance of meaning at work. In one experiment, he brought participants in and described to them a situation in which people were paid to create Bionicles; Lego robot toys. One group created Bionicles in a "meaningful" condition. Besides being paid to create them, they were asked to line them up in a row in front of them so they could see all they had produced. Another group created them in a Sisyphic condition. They were paid to build the Bionicles, but researchers dissembled each Bionicle and dumped the pieces back in the bucket the minute they were built.

Ariely asked the students involved in the experiment how they thought the differences in the two conditions would affect productivity. They estimated that the people in the "meaningful" condition would build one more Bionicle than those in the Sisyphic condition.

As it turned out, the people in the "meaningful" group created four more Bionicles than those in the other group. His participants had underestimated the impact of meaning by 4X.[14] How much are organizations underestimating the importance of meaning?

For the sake of their own productivity, profitability and growth, organizations need to find out what their employees are about. What gets them up in the morning? Surveys won't do it. They take people's temperature at the moment, but they don't ask the deeper questions. Human potential is in the deeper questions. We need a process for understanding, and co-creating, meaning.

THE HUMAN FUGUE

I was introduced to Bijoy Goswami by a client in the late '90s. My partner, Jay, and I met with Bijoy and his partner, Bruce, to talk about recruiting for his startup. Our first meeting, at his Austin apartment, was mostly business. While I was there I noted that he had symbols and models on the whiteboards in the kitchen, and there was even one painted on the floor in his dining room. After we left, I had no idea why my client thought I had so much in common with Bijoy. Six months later I ran across Bijoy's reading list online and noticed we had read many of the same books. I called Bijoy and asked if he had read *The Self-Aware Universe*.

That began a dialogue that has spanned more than a decade.

Bijoy is a model maker. Making models is a way to visualize and clarify how you, and others, define reality. These can be used as different lenses that help us separate ideas and behaviors into useful categories for effective decision making. A simple example might be to think of a lake. A model would allow us to look at the lake through the lens of a cartographer, a park ranger, an angler, a swimmer, a microbiologist, and so forth. One might focus on the lake's geological history, another on its contribution to the ecosystem, and another on how slimy and cold its muddy banks feel. They're all talking about the same lake, and likely having a different experience of it as they view it through different lenses.

Bijoy's model, *The Human Fugue*, provides lenses for understanding several huge domains that encompass much of human existence. He calls these domains houses. They are the houses of phenomena, rights, resources, and meaning.

A key insight in Bijoy's model is realizing that each of these houses has undergone, or is undergoing, a fundamental shift from operating as an authoritarian system to a system with a process that lets individuals participate independently. Authorities in these houses were/are usually small groups or institutions that say: "You don't need to think or participate, we will tell you what to do; we will tell you how things are." When people live in authority-based houses, they are expected to live in the cave, keep the chains on, and accept the reality as defined by the authority — obey, believe and do what you are told. Authorities have their place, but for most functioning adults, in most circumstances, authorities limit or even eliminate the opportunity and impetus for responsibility, intelligence, and creativity.

By contrast, a process enables the individual to be the prime mover. It gives them the opportunity to fix or improve things, but it also requires them to expend the energy to participate, learn the system they're navigating, contribute to the questions, answers, activities, and knowledge in that house. A process allows for myriad mistakes in pursuit of the greater importance of empowering people to act on their own behalf and the behalf of others. In the business context, they act on behalf of their own growth, the success of the organization, and the service of the customer.

We live in an information-rich world with complex sets of interactions and very little clarity around many issues. A process gives us a better chance, collectively, at arriving at a truth. At the same time, processes can be challenging because they are designed to accommodate constant change, and rightly so. Whenever we begin to settle in with the static, authoritarian answers for too long, the institution either becomes obsolete or the barbarians charge the gate and overthrow it. The universe is always advancing. Processes require us to stay alert, keep evolving.

In the first three houses, this shift has already taken place in most advanced societies.

The First House—*Phenomena*—encompasses observable facts, occurrences, or circumstances. Historically an institution, like a religion or monarchy, produced explanations for phenomena and people were expected to accept those explanations. Galileo was among those punished for contesting that system when he wrote that the Earth revolved around the sun. His book *On Motion*, written largely between 1589 and 1592, gave us an initial process for observing and testing phenomena, called the scientific method. By the 1600s, the scientific revolution was underway as any individual could participate by conducting tests on different phenomena. The result is a fact or theory.

The Second House—*Rights*—is a society's legal principles for freedom and entitlement for citizens. People have always had a sense of the value of freedom and justice but little opportunity to exercise it in many historical contexts. Before the American Revolution, rights had almost always been conveyed by a governmental authority and just as easily rescinded or changed. But through the 30-year period between the writing of the Declaration of Independence and the dubbing of the Supreme Court as having the power to rule on what is constitutional, Americans stepped out from under the rule of a king and began a process by which nearly any citizen, acting on their own behalf, could advocate for their rights or the rights of others. The result is a law.

The Third House—*Resources*—includes raw material, energy, or other assets used to satisfy wants and needs. Historically, people could toil for a lifetime and never accumulate wealth because it was firmly in the grip of a minority. Society needed a way to free the creative nature of citizens to create value and exchange resources, so our ingenuity and effort, rather than the favor of a monarch, could determine our financial success. Entrepreneurship enables everyone—particularly today—to identify a problem or opportunity in the market, create a solution, sell it, repeat. The result is a business model.

The transition of the Fourth House—*Meaning*—is happening now. Historically we have vested the power of ascribing meaning to religions and other institutions. But many forces, including the Age of Reason, scientific and technological forces, and increased cultural awareness, have changed that. With no clear authority for meaning, people have begun seeking meaning for themselves, according to their own definitions.

Since we're still in the process, we still have kinks to work out. We think of meaning as an abstract set of aspirations, for example, when it's actually something that can change our behavior and impact our health. We are only just beginning to discern the differences between our authoritarian allegiances to what we've been told is meaningful and what actually moves us.

This presents a conundrum for the organization. Because while employees know precisely what they're getting paid, what their expertise is, and where they rank in the hierarchy, they have

MEANING	JOurneY, Essence Mining	
RESOURCES	Capitalism	
RIGHTS	Democracy	
PHENOMENA	Scientific Method	

1500 1600 1700 1800 1900 2000 2100 2200 ...

THE HUMAN FUGUE
Authority to Process

little or no understanding of how their most human aspect—the things that matter most to them about their work—is being served in the organization. Many give up seeking engagement or fulfillment in the workplace, which renders the hours of their working day a dead zone, both for them and for the organization.

The houses of *Phenomena, Rights,* and *Resources* are so intertwined in our daily lives and thinking that we often forget we're dealing with different domains. This leads to confusion and frustration. In the context of a normal business, someone who wants to leave the company because they don't find their work meaningful might be prevailed upon to stay by the offer of more money, even though the two have nothing to do with each other and the increase in pay only temporarily mitigates the problem. The Human Fugue model calls this "House Confusion."

It's a bit like detangling a ball of necklaces. While they're all

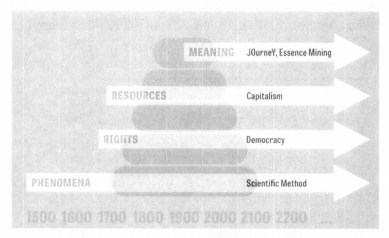

MASLOW'S HIERARCHY IN RELATION TO HUMAN FUGUE

jumbled together, it's hard to understand what you're dealing with. But as you free each one from the others, your understanding of what made up this tangled ball becomes clearer. Looking at business this way is the same. You look at what you're trying to accomplish and ask "Is this *Phenomena*? *Rights*? *Resources*? Or is this *Meaning*?"

Meaning doesn't fit in the logical processes most businesses are accustomed to operating by. A phenomenon can be judged by the number of times it is proven to turn out the same way. A right can be judged by the number of people it serves; a resource can be evaluated in terms of its exchange. But meaning is subjective, personal, and experiential and can't be quantified that way. Rights aren't resources. Every new breakthrough in science isn't something that can be bought or sold. And meaning isn't for sale.

Ever since Bijoy shared the Human Fugue model with me, it has given me a lens through which to see how people often confuse money for meaning, or resources for rights, and other misperceptions. I've used it so often I unconsciously "place" things in houses when absorbing new information.

Until organizations learn to do this, to deal with the fundamental realities of meaning on its own terms, the problem of meaning will continue to grow as a source of disconnect. Individuals seldom know how—or have the power—to solve the problem for themselves in their roles within an organization. As anthropologist Edward T. Hall said in his book *Beyond Culture*:

> *Bureaucracies have no conscience, no memory, and no mind. They are self-serving, amoral. [...] Paradoxically most bureaucracies are staffed with conscientious, committed people who are trying to do the right thing but they are powerless (or feel powerless) to change things...*[15]

And so people disengage, often descending into an existential despair that their lives are meaningless. It is only when they begin to find their own meaning internally, and manifest it in the organization, that they come alive again. As Steve Jobs said:

> *When you grow up you tend to get told that the world is the way it is and your life is just to live your life inside the world. Try not to bash into the walls too much. Try to have a nice family life, have fun, save a little money.*

That's a very limited life. Life can be much broader once you discover one simple fact: Everything around you that you call life was made up by people that were no smarter than you. And you can change it, you can influence it [...] Once you learn that, you'll never be the same again.[16]

Organizations can't give meaning, they can only create an environment in which individuals can be their own prime movers in a meaning process. This process can't be managed and measured like the logical processes of the other three houses and needs its own metrics—one of which is the success of the company.

The need to actualize is becoming a cultural phenomenon. Throughout history, there have been those who moved away from institutions and struggled to assume responsibility for their own meaning, tap the essence of who they are. They have used philosophy, psychiatry, psychology, yoga, and meditation. One by one, people are slipping off the chains, turning away from the cave wall, and crawling out into the sunlight to realize their true potentials for the first time. But it's not happening en masse, because we've been caught up in an authoritarian mindset around meaning. Organizations have had no process for bringing meaning into the organization in the very personal, multifarious configuration that true meaning requires. To offer such a process is to help people access the deepest gifts they have, germane both to themselves and the organization.

But first, we have to look at what meaning is.

Listening Experience: **Who You Are - Pearl Jam**

CHAPTER 5

JOURNEY

So what is meaning?

Meaning is the way we interpret our experiences and engage with our existence.

Many things can be called meaningful, but each of us has a set of beliefs or practices that tap our emotions, command our focus, and engage our determination. That kind of personal, core meaning is visceral. It's so deeply ingrained that it can alter our immune systems.

In 2013, a team led by Steven Cole of the UCLA School of Medicine and Barbara Fredrickson of the University of North Carolina, Chapel Hill studied the physiological impact of meaning. The researchers asked subjects whether they saw their lives as more meaningful (focused on something greater than themselves) or more happy (focused on pleasurable experiences). The happiness we get from following a path we believe to be meaningful is known as eudaimonic happiness; it's different from happiness that comes from seeking rewards or pleasure, which is known as hedonic happiness. The kind of happiness we experience causes our immune systems to change, by alerting them as to the kinds of health risks we are likely to encounter in the future.

The researchers discovered that the people with meaningful lives had immune systems braced to combat viruses that come from contact with lots of people. Conversely, pleasure seekers' immune systems show preparation for ailments involving inflammation, such as heart disease and some cancers. Interestingly, pleasure seekers' immune systems look just like those of people experiencing chronic adversity, such as extreme poverty or abuse.[17] Meaning isn't just an abstract idea, it actually makes us healthier.

HOW MEANING IS CREATED

Does meaning just exist, in an a priori state that we discover, or do we create it? Jung's answer to this question was "both."

Jung recognized a phenomenon in his patients that he called "the collective unconscious." It's similar to parts of an operating system, or core programs, or, as Jung put it, "deposits of the constantly repeated experiences of humanity." Across cultures, you can find the idea of a shaman, one who provides wisdom and insight, an intermediary between the known and unknown. You might call this person a priest or priestess, medicine man, thought leader, or any of a number of other titles. But regardless of where you are or what language you speak, the idea or pattern of such a person is already embedded in your programming, even if you have never met someone like this. This is Jung's "Archetype of the Wise Old Man" whose job it is to help humans surpass the limitations they currently perceive in themselves, to rise up, to become what they're capable of. Think of Mr. Miyagi in *The Karate Kid*, Gandalf in *The Lord of the Rings*, Merlin in *The Sword in the Stone*. In real life we have Gandhi, Jiang Ziya, the Dalai Lama.

In Jung's day, the idea of the collective unconscious was

considered mysticism. Many people preferred the tidier theories of Freud and the behaviorists who treated people, in many ways, like biological robots. It was believed at the time that the human brain was pretty much fixed after childhood. Specific bits of the brain did specific tasks, and one had only to program the right ideas and behaviors into the brain. It's an approach that is still embedded in many of our organizations and institutions today. Jung's theories were much more involved.

So—as it turned out—is our reality.

As neuroscientist David Eagleman points out in his book *Incognito: The Secret Lives of the Brain*:

> *Your brain is built of cells called neurons and glia— hundreds of billions of them. Each one of these cells is as complicated as a city. And each one contains the entire human genome and traffics billions of molecules in intricate economies. [...] The cells are connected to one another in a network of such staggering complexity that it bankrupts human language and necessitates new strains of mathematics.*[18]

So much for tidy packages and easily programmed human beings.

Modern neuroscientists still haven't identified the mechanisms of meaning. But they can tell us that our brains are unique as snowflakes. And that we store things we find meaningful in a group of brain parts known as the limbic system, which is the primary processor of long-term memory, emotion, motivation, and learning. The limbic system is often the deciding factor in any decision having to do with internal states. (Do I want cake? Do I want this job? Do I want to work late on this project?)

People with damaged limbic systems can't make even the simplest decisions. Logic and data alone aren't enough.

The limbic system moves a lot faster than the neocortex, the part of the brain in charge of things like language and abstract thought. Our limbic brain falls in love with a person or a car or a job first, leaving the neocortex to justify its decision with logic and data. In moments of danger, it collects sensory information through the thalamus and alerts the amygdala, which causes us to act without conscious thought. One day I was driving in the right-hand lane when someone from the left-turn lane, obscured in front of a large truck, pulled out immediately in front of me. I don't even remember seeing the car pull out, but I swerved and missed it by maybe an inch. I had no idea how we didn't hit each other. It wasn't until later, after the danger passed, that my rational brain had a chance to sort out what happened.

The limbic system is one of the chief architects of what we believe, because anything that triggers our emotions embeds much deeper in our memories, explained neuroscientist Andrew Newberg at a Pew Forum on faith:

> [The] *amygdala* [...] *tends to light up whenever something of motivational importance happens to us. The hippocampus* [...] *helps to regulate our beliefs, but also helps to regulate our emotions and write into our memories the ideas that come about from emotionally salient events. That is why we all remember exactly what was happening to us on September 11, 2001, but very few of you probably remember what happened on September 10...*[19]

When we experience something particularly vivid or salient, the brain lays down several tracks of memory about what happened. Some information is dumped in the unconscious; some is remembered factually. But when a track of memory is "wired" to the amygdala, a similar experience instantly brings back all the feelings around that original experience, lighting up the amygdala again, alerting us that this new experience, too, is important. "Neurons that fire together, wire together," neuroscientist Donald Hebb famously said. This gives us a form of time travel, according to neuroscientist Endel Tulving, who called this chronesthesia. Experiences or meaningful ideas jump full form into our brain as if we're reliving them. We needn't scroll back chronologically to find them. We can also project these past experiences into the future, playing them out in our minds to help us decide a course of action.

But because experiences that stimulate our limbic areas and resonate with our meaningful memories are so specific to us, they form meaning models that shape our ideas about what reality is and ought to be. Our meaning models are a big factor in how we see ourselves and our role in the universe.

One of my favorite illustrations of this is the Disney/Pixar movie *Inside Out*. In the story, 11-year-old Riley's personality comprises various islands including *"Honesty Island," "Goofball Island,"* and *"Friendship Island,"* each of which contains core memories—playing with her family, connecting with friends—that are narratives in her meaning models. They define her identity. When her circumstances change, her meaning models no longer align with her reality, and she becomes miserable. When the way we're living doesn't align with what we consider important, it conflicts with our sense of self.

That's what happens in disengagement.

SHOES TOO SMALL

Jung's contemporaries treated our unconscious as a sort of psychological discard pile and focused on the ego, which is in charge of regulating our thoughts, emotions, and access to the subconscious and to memory. This is the "I" we're familiar with. The ego, or conscious mind is, as Eagleman said, "like a tiny stowaway on a transatlantic steamship, taking credit for the journey without acknowledging the massive engineering underfoot." We like to think we're in charge. The ego wants to operate as long as possible with as little pain as possible. To do so it represses traumatic memories, as well as thoughts, desires, and behaviors that might get us in trouble. These are tucked into our personal unconscious.

Jung said people suffer from two basic fears: the fear of being abandoned and the fear of being overwhelmed. The fear of abandonment most of us understand. But in my experience it's the fear of being overwhelmed, including the fear of taking personal responsibility for the gold we have to offer—our talents and potential—that is more prevalent. These fears lead us to all kinds of behaviors and feelings we don't particularly want to own, so the ego renames them, redefines them, hides them. It reframes our story so that we can continue to function in our paradigm: family, work, community.

Some of these controls are positive; they help us navigate society. But to deal with the fears or controls that inhibit our growth, we have to unpack them and look at them honestly. To grow, we have to understand how and why we are getting in the way of our own growth, uncover what we are protecting and what wants to be realized. That can be a difficult process for many people.

Hence, as Jung said, we are all "walking around in shoes that are too small for us."

In recent decades, scientists have realized that Jung's theories far more accurately express how our minds work—not as a sovereign conscious with some unconscious junk attached, but both together, with the unconscious doing the lion's share. Jung's ideas about our dreams informing us about the unconscious self have turned out to be accurate. Researchers have studied people's brains while they dream and found that when dreamers wake, the narrative of the dream matches up with the observed brain activity.[20] Dreams let our conscious and unconscious minds work out issues together. Especially during REM sleep, dreaming lets us add new information to old memories to solve problems, weaving unconscious, primal emotions with our conscious thoughts and perceptions. So although we use the term unconscious, it would be more accurate to call it a form of intelligence—one we often struggle to catch up to.

Which brings up another point: Things sent to the unconscious don't stay put. In addition to showing up in dreams, they create stirrings that the ego often represses, resulting in a sense of incompleteness. That explains why someone might like their job, and want to do well, but just can't put their whole heart into it. The ego tells them they've got a good gig. Their neocortex might be shouting praise for the opportunity. But the employee remains unsatisfied, without being able to explain why. We all see this when people in the workplace are constantly reinforcing their enthusiasm. We often think, "Are you trying to convince me, or yourself?"

The collective unconscious, our personal unconscious, and our ego, all weigh in, in their own ways. When it comes to dealing with authority figures, for example, we have archetypal concepts of power from the collective unconscious—the idea of a king, a father or mother—which may impact how we see the person in question. We have our egoic interpretation of power, the convictions and ideas we present as "ours," like, "I have no problem with people being in power over me as long as they're competent." And then we have thoughts, feelings, and perceptions that dwell in our personal unconscious: fear or resentment of people in positions of power. Because these thoughts, feelings and perceptions often conflict with one another, they lead to internal confusion—what Jung called "complexes." Our ego is in conflict with the powerful messages that leak out from our unconscious. Essentially, we are out of sync with ourselves, which leads to anxiety, disengagement, even depression.

Individuation is the process of becoming in sync with ourselves, overcoming this internal conflict, not by choosing one voice over the other, but by synthesizing the creative nature of the psyche and the positive rational approach of the conscious mind into an integrated whole.

Herman Hesse said: I wanted only to try to live in accord with the promptings which came from my true self; why was that so very difficult?

As if in answer, Einstein said: To break a mental model is harder than splitting an atom.

THE WHOLE PERSON, AT WORK

Maslow was looking at people through one lens, the exemplar lens. Jung was trying to help people find their true identities, who they were meant to be, unveiling the powerful world of the unconscious. Both were dealing with the idea of potential: What are people capable of if nothing is holding them back? Not fear, nor complexes, the ghosts of their childhoods, or the unspoken rules of the current society. What could they become? What could they produce if they were psychologically healthy and didn't have to devote energy contorting themselves to maintain their ego projections?

Jim Collins, author of *Good to Great*, had his own lens, the corporate lens, for looking at people who were fulfilling their potentials. He found exemplars he called Level 5 Leaders. These are people who are comfortable with duality and modest about themselves, but fearless about what they're trying to achieve. Maslow said fewer than 2 percent self-actualize. Collins surveyed more than 1,400 companies and found fewer than 11 Level 5 Leaders. That's less than 1 percent. Why?

Fundamentally, the ego developed when we were infants. It seeks stimulation (talking, stroking, holding) gratification (feeding, safety, security) and approval (affirmation that we belong). Because it formed when our very survival depended on the authoritarian system of a nuclear family, it is programmed to perceive what the authority seems to be asking for, so it can keep our thoughts and behaviors in compliance. It sees the unconscious as an anarchist, waiting to take us in unpredictable and dangerous directions. It even makes people fear themselves and their own "shadow" or the things they don't know about themselves. What did that dream mean? We wonder with alarm. What scary things lie within me and what am I capable of? We trust the ego to keep us safe, and the ego trusts the authority.

Most organized cultures work with this paradigm. Leaders often encourage employees to take responsibility for their own contributions — though they might simultaneously create paradigms in which there's little autonomy. Employees don't necessarily trust themselves to take the "right" actions to move the organization forward. So the organization induces the desired behavior through strategies that stroke the ego. They entice employees with bonuses, raises, and perks. They use praise and recognition to provoke people to temporarily improve performance. They tout "best practices" to encourage compliance. And they offer the prospect of autonomy and advancement.

So far, the system's worked, marginally. But as we've learned over time, merely paying people, or involving them in decisions, doesn't satisfy their deepest needs for meaning or the fulfillment of potentials. Nor do many people know how to find work where meaning and fulfillment of potentials is supported. People know the experience of meaning, of their limbic brains being triggered, but they have a difficult time tying it to the tasks of their work. They do know, however, what it is not. And despite the fact that many organizations have well-articulated missions and visions, if they don't trigger the employees' limbic brains, if they don't inspire eudaimonic happiness, they're missing the goal: to tap into the wellspring of commitment, creativity, and resourcefulness that meaningful work elicits.

The people who fuel successful organizations are those who, like Level 5 Leaders, are internally motivated to be their own authorities. Such people don't need extensive and complicated management systems to nurse the ego. They know what matters to them, what they're willing to work for, and, so long as the goal is accessible in their environs, they are motivated to find ways to accomplish it. They are resourceful about getting the job done, rather than requiring resources before getting started. They engage their intelligence, which psychologist and education pioneer Jean Piaget defined as "what you use when you don't know what to do."

Not all people who begin the individuation journey are going to become Level 5 leaders. Some might find that their particular path leads to mastery of a particular skill that doesn't include leadership. But if they were to become their own authorities, and go in search of the potentials that lie within the unconscious, what might they be able to do that they can't do now? Answering that question requires courage.

INDIVIDUATION: THE HERO'S JOURNEY

Potential, by definition, is something not yet manifest. It is a belief that we have an unrealized ability that we haven't tapped, but are capable of tapping. Most of us believe in childhood and youth that we possess unlimited potential. The older we get, the less time we have to take action on it, which causes some to bury it, others to dig in and tap it.

However, most people focus on the daily machinations of life, waiting for the opportunity to present itself while continuing to repress their unconscious thoughts, and growing more and more disengaged from their experience. A person on the periphery of individuating, though, has a moment when the rebel thoughts break out. This may be brought on by traveling to a new place that challenges our ideas of what life should be, by meeting an individuating person, or by the death of a loved one. The experience can jar us, because the beliefs we have clearly don't fit the situation. We look at our beliefs and choices from a new perspective. Questions arise in our minds: Is this who you want to be? Is this how you want to live? It's as if there is "another us" challenging the decision-making paradigm we've been using, and reminding us of someone we used to be, or used to want to be, but have forgotten. Who is this person in our heads who isn't the conscious mind we know? And what are they asking of us? Even if we haven't lived this journey, we all know

73

the story. We've seen it time and again in fiction.

Joseph Campbell's *The Hero's Journey*, a monomyth—or a template for the human journey—that he co-opted from James Joyce's *Finnegan's Wake*, tells of someone who sheds the voices of enculturation, goes deep within the self in the process of pursuing the goal, discovers personal truths, and returns with a gift for the world: the newly discovered, individuated self. Campbell's advice: Answer the call to your own myth.

This template has been used endlessly in movies like *Star Wars*, the *Lord of the Rings* trilogy, and *The Matrix*. After all, humans love stories of struggle, triumph, and personal transformation, perhaps because something in us recognizes the same experience we are called to. The protagonists of these stories have a moment when they see that there is a lot more to the world than their history prepared them for.

This new understanding shakes their ability to keep functioning as usual. The only path forward seems to require facing some great difficulty that puts them at odds with the safety of accepted behavior (since the people around them share the views they now question.) This is the moment when potential is required to become action.

After an internal struggle, they forge ahead and discover that their values or behaviors are inadequate for the task. The characters connect with someone representing the Archetype of the Wise Old Man, the archetype of potential. He is all we are now and all we might become, the culmination of all our possibilities. The Wise Old Man trains them to tap into aspects of themselves they haven't known before—the unconscious, the raw potential—so they can transform themselves, rising to a new level and gaining a different understanding and way of living. This period is always marked by mistakes, failure—ego's arch-nemesis—and a fight to let the unconscious, the potential, the psyche, have its way.

In *Star Wars*, Luke fails miserably at tapping into the Force until he silences his conscious mind, and even afterward the ego rears its head again and again. In *The Matrix*, Morpheus coaches Neo to fight saying: "You're faster than this. … I'm trying to free your mind, Neo. But I can only open the door. You're the one who has to walk through it." And in *The Hobbit*, precursor to *The Lord of the Rings*, Gandalf says of Bilbo Baggins: "I have chosen Mr. Baggins and that ought to be enough for you ... there is a lot more in him than you guess and a deal more than he has any idea of himself."

While most of these stories have "happy" endings, what drives them is meaning. If the characters had wanted to be "happy," they would have stayed on Tatooine, in the Shire, or in the Matrix, where the ego can ensure they make fewer mistakes and are safe in their environment. But as long as they stay where they started, they have no hope of reaching their potential.

Once they do battle with the ego and let the unconscious part of themselves have a say, they become more than they knew they could be. Their new desire becomes to have that experience again and again. People who are individuating know that only through this door of the unknown and fallible self have they found the ability to rise to a new level. They have seen what a miserly ruler the ego is and are no longer satisfied to hide parts of themselves to gain the paltry rewards that come from jockeying for status or winning through manipulation, blame shifting, or posturing. In a work or social situation, this means they present as whole humans, transparent and honest, focused on another "adventure" of potential. They find that any price they paid to gain that freedom makes living authentically that much more valuable. It also makes it that much more important to live life and do work that's meaningful and engages that potential.

STUNTED CULTURES, STUNTED PEOPLE

Jung believed that individuation is the core process of human development and that when people choose to protect their enculturation, rather than individuate, they become stunted. When an entire social group is stunted by its desire to maintain enculturation, Jung said, it's difficult to form viable institutions, which is a critical threat to humanity's potential.

In organizations today, we are seeing more people driven by their desire to maintain their place within the culture than to develop as individuals. Their focus is outward, toward ego validation and personal security. They're playing a role, concealing anything that might reduce their status and fostering hostility toward anything, or anyone, who threatens it. An organization in which everyone is playing their roles creates an illusion of unity and control. But such a culture is weak, relative to what it can be. It rarely produces anything unique. In fact, one of our great social problems today is cultures that support role-playing, conformity, and tribalism rather than individuality. Such cultures are uncomfortable with change and often caught in its crosshairs. So they unintentionally discourage critical thought and innovative thinking, as well as individual growth. And social, cultural, and technological innovation leaves them behind.

New ideas do not, after all, come from homogenous groups protecting the status quo but from distinct identities, discussing, exploring, and subjecting an idea to many viewpoints. They come from people who are internally motivated.

In his book *The Farther Reaches of Human Nature*, Maslow

wrote:

> *I think the problem of the management of creative personnel is both fantastically difficult and important. [...] The kind of creative people that I've worked with are people who are apt to get ground up in an organization, apt to be afraid of it, and apt generally to work off in a corner or an attic by themselves.*[21]

The kind of creative people he'd worked with are self-actualizing people, individuating people, who have to "work off in a corner by themselves" in order to listen to their internal drivers. They get ground up because authoritarian ego controls tell them their value is in how well they fit the prescribed culture, rather than in performing in a way that fulfills their potentials.

Some organizations do manage to create cultures that attract and support individuating people. They open the gates for independent thought, healthy and civil argument, and manifestation of individual character. Maslow believed the right kind of culture could catalyze self-actualization at mass scale and address many of society's ills. Such a culture is what we are working toward by identifying a process for meaning.

In such a company, the organizing principle for getting things done isn't adherence to a cultural norm, but limbic resonance—people whose limbic brains vibrate, as it were, at the same emotional/meaning frequency. People who are united in a meaningful pursuit of the actualization of their potentials. In the work context, this translates into a shared passion for bringing a project, idea, or contract to completion. Limbic resonance builds trust and allows an organization to operate out of its unique identity. Such an organization is in a much better position to weather the tide of automation and replication. That doesn't mean it's an easy task for organizations. None of this is easy, but it's doable if you have a model for doing it.

Much of the work Jung and Maslow did was to help people who had reached a point of crisis in their lives when they were ready to deal with their internal drivers. This can take years. For organizations, the goal isn't to resolve their employees' personal issues, but to address the question of potential at scale. It is up to the individual to decide whether to embark on the journey of individuation, but it is in the organization's interest to foster environments and create the conditions that inspire employees to do the challenging work to tap their potentials. This requires a business-friendly approach.

THE JOurneY MODEL

Jung explained that individuation is a process. He knew that people were drawn to the idea of authoritative meaning systems because of the ego's need for safety and that it was not an easy or instant task to rid the psyche of this inclination. He advocated writing down dreams, using active imagination, and other methods to get in touch with the parts of the Self that have been so long repressed and that are instrumental to individuation. He left us with astounding and brilliant insights but once said of those trying to follow his path: "Thank God I'm Jung and not a Jungian."

Campbell focused on the external story of the hero in which we see the external metamorphosis, but what is being transformed? Bijoy, however, created the JOurneY model (emphasis on JOY) that shows how we internally evolve our meaning models, which may, or may not, be accompanied by external action. We have meaning models for everything, including careers, relationships, metaphysics, and intellect, and each of these has its own journey. They all start with meaning models we inherited.

Stage 1: INHERITED

The narratives in our meaning models are created for us by our families of origin and our culture. What our family was like, how they interacted, what rules and codes predominated, how we interacted with neighbors, our relationship to the cosmos, and so forth. All of these created a meaning model that was given to us by an authority that expected us to adhere to it. Many of our initial meaning models were healthy ways to navigate life; some were not. This is where the ego learned how to behave and what to say to protect us. This is also where it began pushing things into the subconscious, creating our shadow. In our specific environments, there were rules that we learned. But even very young children can get cognitive dissonance when they sense that the rules don't align with something internally. Hence complexes begin.

A Stage 1 organization exists to make money, period. It operates according to Milton Friedman's principle that the "social responsibility of business is to increase its profits." Stage 1 organizations include "cookie cutter" startups that replicate another company's product or service in a different market in hopes of having the financial success of the company they're copying. These organizations do not live very long. Employees often have only a nominal relationship with the organization. When interviewed, they often say: "I work there to make a living. When I get home, that's when I get to be who I am and really live life." These companies have more clock punchers, lots of sick days, and full vacation schedules.

Stage 2: ADOPTED

At some point as individuals, we find that inherited models no longer work for us and new experiences are adding new narratives to our meaning models that seem to work better. Society offers many alternative models to choose from: Some people trade Christianity for Buddhism or Pilates for yoga. We may adopt the meaning models of our school peers, professional associations, or other cultural groups. But these are still authority-based meaning systems, co-opted from someone else. At first, we find them exciting and challenging because we're learning a new way of evaluating and interacting with meaning. We see this in job candidates who leave one place because something isn't working out, so they choose what they perceive as the opposite. The problem is that this creates endless looping in an attempt to figure out what we want. Many of us go through this process in many areas of our lives, many times. But trying to adhere to a model designed by someone else eventually fails to resonate with the true self.

Organizations in Stage 2 are those whose sense of meaning has lost power to inspire. They may adopt a purpose-driven model to restore meaning. They try to galvanize people around a shared meaning, one they adopted. But since meaning is personal, the organization's model doesn't actually connect people with their work. So employees turn cold toward the organization and begin to poke holes in an ideal the organization can never live up to in the first place. Stage 2 organizations can also end up looping, like JCPenney trying to become Apple, because their Stage 1 models no longer work. This is often initiated by new leaders trying to make their mark on an organization. Or it might be inspired by a change in the market that threatens the organization's viability. It's adopting some new, wholesale culture that seems more in line with what the market is asking for.

Many people and organizations will spend eternities in the second step. They change out one model for the other without ever realizing there is a way to self-author our meaning models.

Stage 3: CURATED

This is when we recognize that it's our responsibility to curate our meaning, to choose what resonates with us and disregard the rest. At Stage 3, we have evaluated ourselves and our perspectives on reality through several models. We have embraced beliefs and aspirations that resonate with who we truly are and discarded those that — often despite our best efforts — don't. We can see ourselves through our current lens and our old lenses. Realizing that what we once believed is nothing more than a model, a lens for reality, frees us to be creative about making a new lens that can hold paradoxical truths. It also fosters empathy for others' perspectives.

As we see that our potentials might not be as limited as we thought they were, we begin to stretch them. This is far more fun and interesting than putting forth an image to cover our perceived inadequacies. We become more interested in becoming masters than in appearing to be masters by not taking risks. Our core motivation is to continue to learn and evolve. As we do so, our model of what is meaningful constantly evolves as well because we are open to learning. We constantly identify new meanings and potentials. This is Jung's individuation, Imago Dei, Archetype of the Self. Maslow called it self-actualization, transcendence, or peak experience. It could also be called self-authoring meaning.

This is not individualism. Individualism causes people to focus on their idiosyncrasies as a badge of merit. Individualists compare their uniqueness with that of others as a sort of egoic hierarchy or competition. They are focused on how their contribution will be perceived by others.

An individuating person is curious about what they can contribute from their more authentic selves, but their focus is more on their ability to contribute to something greater than to gain attention for that contribution. It's more like a musician in the orchestra, trying to get the best possible performance from themselves in pursuit of the best performance for the orchestra. It seems a subtle distinction, but it's a crucial one. An individuating person can begin to see the uniqueness in everyone better, because they're no longer competing for social standing, but for excellence. Like the orchestral player, they're happy to see the oboist, the cellist, and the bass drummer do well because they're not threatened by their success or unique contribution. Their focus is on the work, the shared meaning, not on themselves.

A Stage 3 company stewards its meaning by focusing on its customers and the meaning journey of its employees. It constantly focuses on who it is and what it does best, which can sometimes lead to new markets and products. Everyone is a steward of organizational meaning. Companies like Apple don't get stuck, from what I can tell, in a meaning that worked for them in the past. Instead, they continue to explore other avenues— like evaluating billion-dollar markets they haven't entered. If the direction doesn't fit who they are, though, they walk away, regardless of the billions they could have made. They are an organization on a journey filled with people who are also on a journey. Employees' relationship with the company is a healthy immersion. They don't see their identities as wrapped up in the company, but the company is a place where they all believe they can contribute to something bigger than themselves.

What unites people in a Stage 3 organization isn't a motto, a chant, or even a culture enforced from above. What unites them is what unites all people trying to accomplish something powerful that involves collaborating: shared meaning.

Listening Experience: **The Humbling River - Puscifer**

CHAPTER 6

WHO ARE YOU?

When businesses talk about an organizational journey, they're thinking in terms of market shifts, new products and services, growth, and expansion. They don't consider that the organization has a meaning journey, too, which will proceed whether the organization stewards it or not. What the organization is about needs to evolve, along with how it addresses changes in the market, technology, trade, and everything else.

A Stage 1 company that exists solely to make a profit doesn't consciously take a meaning journey, of course. Milton Friedman, a big proponent of the idea that a business's only responsibility is to make a profit, once wrote that businesses could not have responsibilities, only people have responsibilities. A corporation, he said, is an "artificial person,"[22] inferring that it has an identity but not a personality. A Stage 2 organization doesn't consciously take a meaning journey either. It attempts to supply it as if meaning were something static, intended for an "artificial person." But artificial people don't work for an organization—real people do. Like real people, organizational meaning is not static, it evolves. And we have to account for this fact.

This is the point that Arie de Geus, former head of Shell Oil's Strategic Planning Group, addressed in his book *The Living*

Company. De Geus argued that an organization is a living being because, unlike an inanimate thing that can only be acted upon, it acts toward its own purpose. And that is what allows it to live and grow.

When Shell turned 100, de Geus related, it looked around for other long-lived companies for insight on what made a company thrive for a century. It found only 30, ranging in age from 100 to 700 years old. The average lifespan for a corporation in Japan and Europe is 12.5 years. Fortune 500 multinationals generally last 40 to 50. Why can't companies just keep going once they're established? It's not because of changing markets. Many of the companies de Geus studied—including Shell itself—had changed markets and entire industries several times.

But the short-lived organizations focused exclusively on profit. The longest-lived organizations didn't. They focused on the human community that made up their organizations. They adapted to the changing environment because they were not static entities in which people were merely assets; they were living companies. De Geus cited psychologist William Stern, inventor of the IQ test, as saying that institutions and groups of people have personas. A persona, Stern said, is goal-oriented, wanting to "live as long as possible and realize the development of its potential from its talents and aptitudes." It is conscious of itself as an "I", even though it comprises parts and elements that have their own personae. It is in constant relationship to the outside world, and has a finite lifespan.[23]

An organization that stewards its meaning journey can flex, grow, and become more. An organization with a static meaning is stunted. It will develop in unhealthy ways and eventually fail altogether. That's a key reason many people have 14 jobs by the time they're 40.

Of course, some people don't know what they're looking for, or running from. But there are many others, committed people who want to be in an organization where they can forge deep relationships while expanding their potentials. They want to be part of building something that matters, with people who share their passion. They also want to grow and differentiate. If they run into a static meaning model, they will quickly leave the job behind like the shell of a hermit crab.

This behavior is costly. Wooing new people who are less developed than the ones the company just lost consumes a lot of unnecessary energy. It costs an exorbitant amount to continually recruit and onboard. And it drains institutional knowledge, culture, and morale. Then there are the employees who don't move on but are frequently dead wood when it comes to organizational potential because they themselves are not evolving.

They've settled—however unhappily—for a static meaning.

Those are factors all organizations recognize. But there are others they likely don't because they have never had anywhere to put them on a balance sheet. One of these is the fact that people need meaning, and to fulfill their potentials, whether the organization stewards those processes or not. Regardless whether anyone's paying attention to this reality, their limbic systems and unconscious archetypes are the first to push the button on decisions, though employees will secondarily frame arguments to fit the lines of logic and the language of business. In other words, your employees may be unwittingly carrying the organization down a path even *they* don't understand.

Another factor organizations fail to account for is that, while every person in the organization has unrealized potentials, probably only a fraction of that potential is directed toward the work. Their potential is a wasted resource. If you had such a leak of cash, IP, or leadership, you'd do something about it, because you would know the cost to your organization. And you'd have tools to deal with it. But few organizations have even begun to find tools to deal with personal meaning.

Using the lens of the Human Fugue it's clear that the processes of the first three houses are of no use, ruled as they are by logic, analysis, and right and wrong answers. Trying to get a handle on organizational meaning through these houses is like paying someone to fall in love with someone other than their partner, or offering to promote them if they can manufacture a particular kind of dream. They may take the bait, change their behavior temporarily, but their loves and their dreams will remain the same. As Blaise Pascal said:

The heart has its reasons, of which reason knows nothing.

But there is a process by which a living, evolving organization comprising many different people, with all their own evolving meaning models, can be stewarded by the organization. It begins with language—the tool people generally use to share their meaning journeys with each other.

LANGUAGE MAKES CULTURE MAKES LANGUAGE

After Bijoy developed the Human Fugue model, we had long talks about whether to call the areas of knowledge and action he was talking about "domains" or "houses." He advocated for houses, I for domains. Using the wrong word can skew the whole string of inquiry, so we like to get it right. Then I stumbled on an old documentary about Jung. In it, the Rev. Don Cupitt said of Jung:

He thought that scientific, industrial man suffered great

psychic distress and frustration because the religious side of our nature is repressed [...] it's through religion that we work out a common vocabulary of rituals and symbols that together make up a House of Meaning that we dwell in, our particular vision of the universe, of human life, of relationships and so forth.[24]

House was the correct term. There might be different domains within a particular house, but the term "house" captures each space correctly. House of Meaning is where we shape cultures. Where is the organizational House of Meaning? Not in a religion, but in a "common vocabulary of rituals and symbols" that contain our particular vision of the universe. The way we share this vision with other people in the organization is through language.

The idea that language can impact the workplace isn't new. Marvin Bower used language in the 1950s when converting McKinsey & Co. from a run-of-the-mill accounting firm into a prestigious consulting firm. Bower had no interest in running an accounting firm, according to Duff MacDonald, author of *The Firm: The Story of McKinsey and Its Secret Influence on American Business*:

In Bower's mind accountants were drones bound by rules while consultants were free thinkers whose vision and creativity extended far beyond balance sheets. [...] (Bower's) abiding goal was to invent a new profession to prepare clients for the challenges and uncertainties of an onrushing future.

So Bower worked to create a corporate culture that would empower his workforce to meet this mission. There was a dress code. There was a code of conduct. And there was a language.

They had "clients" rather than customers. They played a "role" rather than having a job. They were a "firm" with "members" rather than a company with customers. Along with the other markers of the culture he developed, Bower's language shaped an identity for McKinsey that directed the organization's future and defined the experience of its clients and consultants.[25]

That use of language, though, is far less powerful than it was in the 1950s when employees expected employers to be paternalistic and give them an identity. Employees today see themselves more as free agents seeking an authentic connection. Moreover, the workplace is far less homogenous, with far more women, three generations and people from many countries and cultures working together. Many efforts to better wield language for cultural cohesion begin with huge assumptions (think about all those articles on how to communicate with Millennials, Gen Xers, Baby Boomers) or involve words that different people define quite differently.

A study published in 2007 in the *Journal of Brand Management* investigated whether employees had to personally buy in to a brand for it to succeed. Turns out they do. Marketing researchers Ceridwyn King and Debra Grace interviewed employees about how connected they felt to the brand of the organizations they worked for. While some were connected, others said such things as:

> *They do a lot of training and try to get everyone thinking the same way.*
>
> *When you leave one firm and go to another [...] there is only so much you can read about and often things are written the way people want them to be and not the way they really are.*[26]

In other words, when people didn't resonate with a company's message or language, they felt manipulated by the effort to get them "thinking the same way." Generally, the message used to attract both employees and customers to the brand is created by the marketing department, or an outside consultant, based loosely on a perceived culture, as well as on a clever message it hopes will connect or inspire by activating people's limbic brains.

But marketing is a language used to generate awareness to buy a product or a service—the third house—and reflects what you offer the marketplace right now. It has a direct financial objective. If the campaign doesn't work, you change the message. Meaning can't just be swapped. And if the message is misaligned with the employee's experience, the employee won't just be disengaged; they'll be cynical. That, as King and Grace pointed out, has a profoundly negative impact on the brand overall.

Organizations have tried to create meaning languages the same way they use the language of the first three houses, where concepts are understood and unchanging: product, market, asset, R&D, opportunity cost, succession plan. We have spent centuries creating and refining these languages. Once we learn them, we can easily communicate goals and tactics to reach them and operate in unison. It's like the story of the Tower of Babel: Because everyone spoke the same language, they were united in building a tower that reached to heaven and creating a name for themselves. God's way of thwarting this presumption was to change all their languages so they couldn't understand each other. Sure enough, the people scattered and the project was abandoned.

With the shared languages of the first three houses, we've been able to reach great heights in terms of discovery, prosperity, and creating a system for a functioning society. But when it comes to meaning language, the words—freedom, commitment, autonomy, social good, change, innovation—have myriad meanings. An asset is an asset no matter where you go; it has a legal definition. But what about freedom? An affluent, suburban Millennial from Silicon Valley might have a set of beliefs, values, and aspirations around the idea of freedom that would differ completely from someone on an engineering team in Mumbai. A Generation X military veteran raised in the rural South might have a set of associations totally different from the first two.

Because each person's experience defines how they see freedom, they might speak of it very differently, have different stories illustrating it, and have to work to find common ground around the concept of freedom. But odds are they won't spend a lot of work time talking about it because it doesn't seem like the kind of conversation you're supposed to have on the clock. So they accept a definition that doesn't actually inspire any of them and are, like the Babylonians, scattered, unable to come together to create amazing things fueled by a shared idea of meaning.

This stunts the organizational ability to become a living company that can evolve. As Arie de Geus said:

> *Language creates reality [...] The language that we use when we speak to one another in our companies, creates the reality that we face inside those companies. If we talk about the company as an asset-based, profit-producing machine, we create a different reality than when we see a company as a living thing, a community of people. Talking about companies in the language of a human community may make us see the corporate reality in a way that can help solve problems resulting from our previous views.*[27]

So what is the language of the human community of people? It's a meaning language. One that has yet to be developed in most organizations. It's not a static meaning language, any more than human meaning is static. It's fluid, and personal.

David Whyte, an English poet of Irish extraction, is often hired to speak to corporate leaders. This may seem like an odd gig for a poet. In fact, he thought it was an odd gig when someone first suggested it to him 20 years ago. In a radio interview, he recounted how he was signing books one day when an American wearing a suit arrived at the front of the line.

"We have to hire you," he said.

"For what?" Whyte wanted to know.

"The language we have in the (corporate) world is not large enough for the territory we have already entered," the man said. "And in your language I've heard a language large enough."

The territory he was talking about was "the territory of human relationship that the workplace was entering," Whyte said, "the movable human relationship."[28]

Organizational leaders, Whyte points out, are usually people who are promoted out of their core technical competency and into a job that's about human relationships. When they rely on the language they used in that core competency the message is garbled, like the tangled ball of necklaces. A meaningful conversation demands a different vocabulary, and a different approach, based perception and experience. Having this kind of conversation transforms the company, leaving the "artificial person" behind.

It helps the organization evolve.

WHAT DO YOU MEAN?

But a culture is not just contained in the stories that one hears its members recount. It is also in the encounters that make the tellings possible, in the types of organization that allow people to participate or be left out, be competent or incompetent, give orders or execute them, ask questions or answer them. [...] to be an ethnographer of language means to have the instruments to first hear and then listen carefully to what people are saying when they get together. It means to learn to understand [...] what counts as meaningful for them [...] to divide the continuous flow of experience that characterizes one's perception of the world into manageable chunks...[29]

— **Linguistic anthropologist Alessandro Duranti**

I used to think a lot about the content of conversation and give language little heed. But I've since realized how significant it is that two people can use the same word and mean something totally different. This was a key discovery. A hiring manager might say the organization was committed to employee development and growth and the candidate would hear those words and overlay their ideas of development and growth, learning only later that they weren't talking about the same thing at all.

Just as each of us has a personal meaning model with narratives to explain it, we also have a personal meaning language. It's full of symbolic terms and abstract ideas that can only be clearly understood in the context of our narratives and our unique way of speaking. At every inflection point, a nuance in the way people used words could make an enormous difference in their ability to connect to what matters. People may have similar narratives, but because they use different words to explain them, they think there's a disconnect. Or they may have different narratives but use the same word, growing increasingly frustrated when this "shared idea" manifests so differently from what they expected.

A big part of this is in our vernaculars. We all have vernaculars that come from our families of origin, our region, our social groups, our professional background. "Truth," for a journalist, for example, means they have their facts straight and they've identified something through evidence, whereas truth for a philosopher refers to an underlying principle of the universe that may have little evidence except in how it resonates within us. Both "truths" are valid, but if they're used interchangeably, serious misunderstandings can occur.

Navigating vernacular differences can be tricky between people who are different and even trickier between people who are similar. Because of the things they share in common, two similar people are likely to make all kinds of assumptions about what the other person is saying, without examining it at all. That may explain why diverse teams are more productive. They take less for granted.

That is why, as Rev. Cupitt paraphrased Jung, it is important for people, in this living, human relationship to "work out" a House of Meaning together, rather than having it assigned and losing much of the import and nuance that makes this meaning actually meaningful.

Gary Erickson, CEO and founder of Clif Bar, had a brilliant VP of Human Resources who understood this concept. In 2002, Clif came up with *Five Aspirations* to express its business model: *Sustaining our Business, Brands, People, Community,* and *The Planet.* Five years later, Erickson knew they needed to more deeply embed the culture. So he met with executives and outlined four things that he thought were crucial in how employees showed up every day.

After he presented his thoughts at a meeting, and before he could get to the door, the VP of Human Resources tackled him.

"Wait," she said. "Before we do that, I think it's really important to know the essence of the organization. If we just go out there with values and ideas that don't embody what our people value, it's going to be a real uphill battle. If we have an agenda that doesn't connect to the employees and that isn't meaningful to them, it won't work. Why don't we mine what is already great?"

So they did. Instead of telling the employees what the values were, they asked. They began a conversation, paying specific attention to the language everyone was using and how it related or diverged. It produced what Clif calls its five ingredients: *Create. Inspire. Connect. Own It. Be Yourself.* For example, some of the statements to explain what *Be Yourself* means to employees include *"Don't check your values or your personality at the door"* and *"Develop a level of self-awareness, recognizing both strengths and self-development areas."*

The employees and Clif were on a journey together and they created a language to define and describe it, together. I don't know whether Clif's language has evolved since then. But I do know that continuing to foster these kinds of conversations and allowing the language and culture to evolve is the only way it can thrive.

I also know many leaders fear that opening such a dialogue means plunging into a mire of people's personal emotional discharge that has nothing to do with KPIs or getting the work done. They feel unqualified to dive into people's meaning and worried that it will drag them away from the work at hand. I would feel the same way if what was being proposed was a big feelings-fest, but it isn't. I'm not interested in being anyone's therapist, but I am interested in helping people tap into something inside themselves that helps them deepen their connection to work in a way that benefits the organizations they are part of. I'm interested in people taking advantage of the opportunity they have to steward their meaning and the organizational meaning. I'm interested in helping to create living companies. Living companies are more sustainable and make more profound contributions to humanity and the communities we live in. We need a lot more of them. This is why it is imperative to develop processes to help organizations tap the creative potential of their employees and to drive a sense of connectedness back into the work that so many have lost touch with or taken for granted.

Actually, there's an innate structure for meaning language that makes that easier.

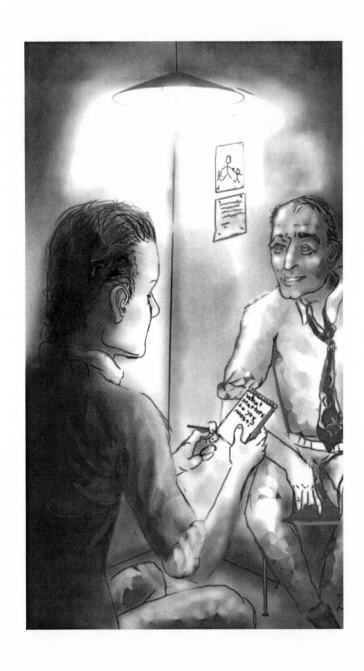

Listening Experience: **Schism - Tool**

CHAPTER 7

ESSENCE MINING

Early in the 20th century, Carl Jung did a study with another Swiss psychiatrist, Franz Riklin, about how people's unconscious symbols manifested in their language. They used word association. What they discovered is that when people were alert, their words matched in meaning. So with the word "bloom" they might associate "flower." But when they were sleepy, or in some other way less alert, they matched words on phonetics. With "bloom" they might say "bloomer."

At first, Jung and Riklin thought the phonetically matched words had no symbolic connection. But after many studies, they looked at the pools of words collected from each subject. And it turned out that, when you look at them all together, they fall into a symbolic category that you would never see unless you were looking for the connections. So if you think of bloom as a flower and bloomer as an article of clothing, with no apparent connection, the rest of the words revealed that they both belong to a family of subconscious symbols connected with sex. Now while Freud associated nearly every psychological concept with sex, Jung did not. In fact, the pool of words might all connect around death, love, family, or some other thing. But invariably they built a host of meaningful connected words around the one the researchers started with. It wasn't random.

Another language expert who discovered almost the same thing was linguist Theodore Thass-Thienemann, author of the 1973 book *Interpretation of Language.* Thass-Thienemann wrote that people have a variety of meanings and that, in each meaning, one central idea is reflected, but surrounded by supporting ideas. The central idea is usually an emotionally loaded concept. In other words, meaning language has a structure we're not conscious of when we're talking.

I found the exact same pattern when interviewing people. They had narratives and symbols, a whole unconscious and conscious vocabulary around what was meaningful to them that they'd never consciously tied to the work they did. But once we began to parse those narratives, like separating the individual necklaces, they began to understand in a whole new way what they were looking for from life, and what they really wanted to work for.

INNOVATING THE INTERVIEW: THE EARLY DAYS

When I started the new company under my first recruiting employer, I had to figure out how to recruit in the technology space and how to train recruiters. It usually takes a recruiter several years to become proficient, and the language of tech was new for all of us. I wanted to shrink the learning curve and get my recruiters a lot of experience, fast. Traditional recruitment training focuses on walking a candidate through a process toward placement. Over time, recruiters gain a more nuanced understanding of what happens in each phase, until, as an experienced recruiter, they can pick up much more quickly where a candidate is in their personal development and what's driving them. This seemed like a skill my team could master if they really understood people and their core drivers. But to get at the essence of what the individual was about in a short amount of time we had to interrogate and challenge their motives and their decision-making paradigms.

I committed every day to tinkering with the traditional interviewing framework. I read everything I could get my hands on about interviewing: interrogation techniques, how to spot a liar, psychological interviewing tactics, and so forth. As we developed the interviewing framework, some patterns began to emerge in how to get to the heart of motive.

We started by asking candidates to tell their stories: past, present, and future, from Day 1, Breath 1. Most people let their ego drive when it comes to talking about their career decisions. Often the ego only recalls what is useful to its continued survival. One way to help interviewees break through old programs they've been running—both positive and negative—is to have them get into storytelling mode. When the recruiter is curious, and willing to challenge the key decisions the candidate has made in life, the candidate begins to see their patterns, and become empowered to change them. What experiences did they choose or were they attracted to? And where did they hope to go from there? We listened for keywords and common refrains that ran through their lives.

In addition to all the techniques we were weaving into the interviewing framework, I built a series of questions around each category of Maslow's hierarchy to ascertain what needs they were looking to fulfill. What did they hope to accomplish? Did they seek out social acceptance? How did they plan to fulfill unmet needs? This could be gleaned from how they talked about their experiences. I also used Jung's archetypes loosely, trying to ascertain what story they might be living out. Was it their own or their parents'?

> *What did you want to be when you grew up?*
>
> *What was your idea of life or career when you started school? When you finished?*
>
> *What attracted you to your first job?*
>
> *What did you like about it?*
>
> *What was your mindset about the business model, peers, superiors, etc.?*
>
> *Did the job turn out to be as you expected?*
>
> *What was different?*
>
> *What are you looking for in the dialogue between you and your workmates or leaders?*

We could use this technique to interrogate meaning as well as to bypass a lengthy process teaching recruiters all of the technical terms. Since we weren't tech experts ourselves, we honed in on the way candidates talked about their skills, breaking each skill down to its fundamental function, just like we had the motivations. For example, if they told us they had written the Java code for a project, we would ask what parts of the project were their responsibility. Did they make decisions or merely follow instructions? How were decisions made? Who else was on the team and what were their roles? What aspects of it did they enjoy, and what aspects were distasteful to them and why?

We began to learn what aspect of the skill engaged them and, hence, where they excelled. We were able to examine that skill in relation to what they contributed to projects they worked on, and how their contribution impacted the project and company.

This gave us a much clearer idea about the type of team on which they might best contribute. We didn't know it back then, but we were examining the relationship (H4) people had with each of the houses, their skills (H1), their reporting relationships (H2), and the business models (H3) they worked in. We were stumbling around the concepts of JOurneY and the Human Fugue before Bijoy had crystallized them.

Recruiters had to break down what candidates were saying and look at them through the various lenses. We called this "Sharing the Picture." It was our job to ask questions that helped candidates paint their picture of what work should look like. How did they resolve core conflicts—for example, between doing what they love or working just for the money?

What did their answers say about where they felt they were on Maslow's hierarchy? What did they say about how they felt about their financial situation, and were they talking about actual dollars or were they talking about their perceived value to the organization? What did they feel like they were missing in their current employment situation and to what "bucket" did it belong? Meaning? Status? Potential? Relationships? Then the recruiter would reflect what they were hearing back to the candidate to clarify whether they were getting an accurate picture of their values, beliefs, and aspirations.

This had a profound impact on the candidate. Having a recruiter listen intently and work to understand them helped them engage more deeply, with trust. As we began to master this framework, our recruiters learned to assess skill competency in multiple disciplines in a matter of months. We got so good at interviewing that we could recommend candidates many recruiters and hiring managers would have ignored. We were also being asked to interview, and give feedback on, candidates other recruiters had found.

Every evening we reviewed the conversations that both trainees and our experienced recruiters had during the day. My team heard hundreds of stories and experiences that each day offered us a deeper understanding of what mattered to people in work and life. When you have 20 people focused on highly engaged conversations, you begin to recognize patterns in the things people say and the way they express themselves. When we hit on an overarching idea we called it a "theme." People might have several themes in their lives. Some of these themes might belong to a person in any industry, profession, company, or level of expertise, such as "I am a perpetual learner" or "I want to do work that makes a difference."

Others seemed specific to certain industries or skill sets. A programmer or software engineer, for example, might espouse themes like "I want to solve hard problems" or "I want to create something new." These themes are like containers of meaning. When you "unpack" that container, you discover unique sets of values, beliefs, and aspirations that support and explain what makes that meaning model important to that person. Often they had a set of experiences and narratives that played into the theme. It was the same pattern as those subconscious pools of meaning Jung, Riklin, and Thass-Thienemann had referenced—a central concept supported by many related concepts.

The themes are crucial, because a group of people inspired by similar themes can generate its own energy. Knowing someone's theme helped identify where they might work best. But I also needed to find a word that aptly categorized the supporting narratives that were diverse, but so consistently present in each theme. I searched through English, Greek, Latin, and German, finally landing on the Sanskrit word "mantra" which means, among other things, "to think in a way that protects and transforms." That was exactly what these related concepts did; protect and transform people's beliefs about their potentials.

Our mantras are beliefs, values, and aspirations around a narrative in our meaning model that we constantly seek to reinforce and evolve. Themes are packed with individual mantras. These are the elemental drivers of the individual and what we seek to uncover in our interviewing process. Mantras can be affirming or negating. It gives greater clarity when people contrast their experiences in different organizations in terms of what worked for them and what didn't.

This deep dive into the candidate made it far easier to give added value and perspective around organizational hiring decisions. The dialogue between recruiter and candidate proved to be essential in helping the company determine what they really needed and who could help them get there. It was a tangible framework for what many thought were intangibles.

We had developed a simple, replicable process for engaging in an essential dialogue with the individual. It made a dramatic difference for their work journey. Using this methodology, we could help people find jobs in places where they would grow, contribute, and strengthen the organization with their presence. The matches made sense in the greater scheme of their narratives, not just on the basis of having a skill that met a job requirement. While much of what we were doing was mined from science books, I wasn't too concerned if it was provable or not. I cared about the fact that it worked. By the time we stopped to look up, we had completely innovated the interview.

While we always spoke about our interviewing framework as a process, we never spelled out the steps of the process. In fact, I think the use of the term "process" was largely unconscious in that it just felt right. We were transforming the organization one person at a time, through a process for meaning in the individual's work journey.

We would soon turn the lens toward the organization—to organizational meaning.

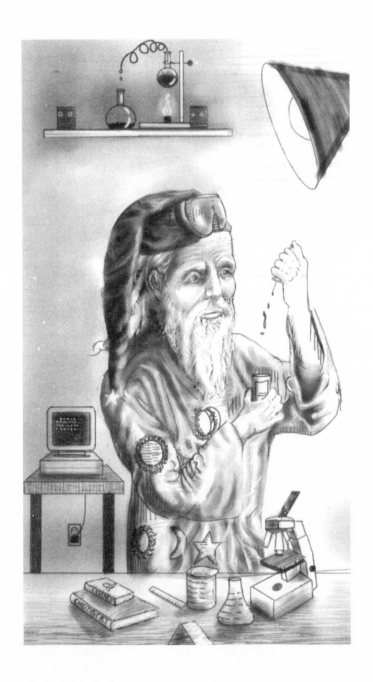

Listening Experience: **The Weaver - Puscifer**

CHAPTER 8

ESSENTIAL DIALOGUE

Jay Long and David Payne were part of my leadership team for the tech recruiting company. We shared a passion for transforming the relationship between people and their work. So in 2005, we launched a company, and we've been on this journey together ever since. Instead of sticking with the technology industry, we decided to focus on physician search.

The traditional recruiting model says that the client pays a recruiter to represent a candidate, and whoever places a candidate in the opening gets paid. This put a price tag on the candidate's head, and I felt it was a fundamental misalignment in motive. It's a model that everyone uses, yet most people I talk to in confidence call recruiters a *"necessary evil."* I thought this needed to change. It ignored the things we considered crucial, like whether the candidate could fulfill their potentials in the job, or whether they would be able to make a meaningful contribution. So we took the price tag off the candidate's head and sought out long-term relationships with clients to provide them with the right candidates, building trust over time.

We also knew we couldn't ignore the role of technology as we built the company.

I had a habit of writing questions on the whiteboard in my

office for everyone in our organization to ponder. One morning in 2008 I wrote: *If we were to put ourselves out of business, today, using technology, how would we do it?*

Normally I posted a new question every few weeks. That one stayed up for more than a year. We ran out of room listing the number of suggestions and new problems it posed. YouTube had opened accessibility to video content as a solution. The vivid, immediate means of communicating a message made sense, but few organizations had begun using it. Jay was emphatic that doctors, talking about the organizations they worked for on video, could impart an authenticity and emotion about the culture that would speak to candidates on a deeper level. We hoped candidates would self-select based on whether the organization resonated with them, rather than just listening to a sales pitch by a recruiter about location or compensation. So we sent Flip cameras and a list of questions to our clients' physician recruiting and marketing departments so they could interview their own physicians and administrators. Then we edited the videos, emailed them to candidates, and posted them on our job board.

Over a couple of years, we collected data on several million interactions—how many times the videos were watched and what actions candidates took when they received them. But the data confused us. Some of the videos were watched repeatedly, others hardly at all, and there was no clear logic as to why some were more popular. It didn't seem related to the charisma of the interviewees or the quality of the videos. We couldn't tie it to geography, size of the town or city, rural vs. urban, size of the institution, or position—all the things that normally determine the desirability of an open position. Why, for example, was the video about the open oncology position in Salina, KS, getting better results than the one in Philadelphia, PA? Knowing what drove these interactions became critical to driving results for our clients. The only thing clear was the videos that were scripted—not authentic—got poor results.

So we devised a matrix that organized videos by types of openings, types of information presented, and the success of the video. I called people from different disciplines to help us identify the differentiators. We also called physicians, nurses, and executives and watched the videos with them online to get their initial reactions. At one point, David called a candidate who was a mid-career breast surgeon, and together they watched a video of a young breast surgeon talking enthusiastically about the hospital where she worked. After a few seconds, the doctor said, "No, stop. Stop."

"What's wrong?" David asked.

"Look," she said. "This doctor is only a few years out of school. She doesn't know what she doesn't know. She can't tell me how to navigate the medical system in that institution compared to other places. I want to hear the truth of that. I appreciate her enthusiasm—she's said 'love' three times in the past three sentences—but I want to hear from someone in mid-to-late career. I also want to hear from hospital leadership."

She wanted social proof from others at her level of experience, and she wanted information she cared about. Our clients had been posting videos of only three to five employees, completely missing the point of connection for many candidates.

It was clear that we were never going to understand the most effective way to create, edit, and post these videos as long as so many factors were out of our hands. The whole process demanded more rigor and consistency than we could get by sending the questions and the camera and hoping for the best.

So I decided to do the next round myself. I called a client, Baptist Health Systems in San Antonio, TX, and asked them to set up 20 people for me to interview from various departments, at different positions, in different locations around town, and with varying amounts of tenure. During the interviews, I kept hearing shared themes. At least two or three connected across the entire organization. This wouldn't have been remarkable if they were parroting something in the recruiting or marketing materials. But they weren't. The ideas they expressed weren't part of the organization's stated culture or written down anywhere. We spoke to a cardiologist who had little or no interaction with a neurologist who worked in a different part of town. They articulated nearly identical themes about what was meaningful to them working at Baptist: how they were able to master their skills, why they believed the organization supported them in doing so. They had different mantras around why their ability to fulfill these themes mattered, but the emotional core of their experiences was the same.

The interviews kept getting longer because once I understood one person's themes and mantras, I would communicate them to the next person I interviewed, their colleague, and they lit up with excitement. They were sharing limbic resonance with people they may have never met in the organization before. The people I interviewed ushered in other employees who were not on the schedule to talk to me. Through asking questions, I was talking these people through the process of exploring organizational meaning. I didn't see all this initially. I was having my own epiphany, seeing how, even in an organization this large, spread across the city, there was a meaning structure and architecture that drove the culture. I could already pick out an identifiable set of motives, values, and aspirations. If this structure existed here, did it exist in other places?

We used our interview framework with other clients we recruited for: Penn State University, the University of Michigan, Expedia. People not only expressed what was meaningful to them about their work, but, in the process of the dialogue, they had new revelations about why they worked there and how their choice to be there made sense in the narrative of their lives. It was transformational. We were unintentionally helping to initiate a meaning competence.

"We always knew this was true about our company," they'd say. "We just didn't think about it this way."

What everyone was experiencing was the power of a process for meaning within the organization. It's lighting the fuse that runs to the powder keg of latent potential.

People spend a lot of time worried that they're in the wrong company, the wrong career, living a life that doesn't align with who they are and what they deeply value. It makes it difficult for them to commit, to invest. But when you can clearly see that you are, in fact, serving what you value in the work you do for an organization, and that the people around you are also serving those values, it's both reassuring and energizing. Realizing that you're not off course or wasting time revives your enthusiasm and gives you confidence to act boldly and decisively. When you realize you're in the right place to tap your potential, you're more likely to do that. The awareness that you share this experience with your coworkers builds camaraderie and trust.

This is what organizations are looking for.

We had also figured out that there was a step-by-step process for the individual worker to uncover and curate their work journey, and a step-by-step process for organizational meaning. This process involves an essential dialogue. I call it Essence Mining. Ken Blanchard, author of *The One Minute Manager*, says it best:

> *There are two parts of collaborating with anybody else. One is essence and the other is form. Essence is heart to heart and values to values and form is how you're going to do it. Be careful in a relationship when someone wants to go to form right away, because if they do that you'll always get bit right in the tail by essence. Essence has got to come first.*[30]

THE CHALLENGES OF ESSENCE MINING THE ORGANIZATION

Essence Mining an organization is difficult for several reasons.

It takes skill to get people to open up on video, to forget the camera is there. And capturing interviews with video is critical. When you're talking to so many people, you forget details. If you use notepads, you are focused on writing. But with videos, you can create a more natural dialogue once the camera is forgotten. Then, when you review the videos, you recognize that many people used the same word or expressed essentially the same idea in different words. Details that seem unimportant become beacons once you've assembled many interviews. Going back over the video interviews several times allows you to pull out the themes that may not have jumped out at first.

Video is also the only tool that can effectively capture meaning for this purpose because of prosody. Prosody is the natural melody of speech: pitch, range, level, rises and falls, loudness, rhythm, tempo. A person's prosodic characteristics reflect their emotional state. Speech speeds up and has more variation during times of happiness; it slows down and has less variation in sadness. Prosody helps us discern what's important and what something means to an individual. It clues your limbic system to levels of engagement. It's also a great B.S. antenna.

Any team leader could Essence Mine their own teams. I do it all the time, but there are drawbacks.

It's tough to mine if you are the boss. People feel less free to discuss what is meaningful in an honest way. While the scope is highly focused, an Essence Miner can't be looking for specific answers. If they are, they will probably find them, or coach them out of people, and completely miss what's most important. When I'm going to Essence Mine a company, I study its structure a month before: What types of activities do they engage in daily? How do they express themselves in marketing or employment literature? What words do they use? Then I push this information to the back of my mind.

I enter the scene full of curiosity that would be considered strange coming from someone in the organization. People expect commonalities and assumptions among coworkers, even if they don't know one another. Because of these assumptions, an internal person is at risk of missing the truth. It's critical to define, define, define, when it comes to what is meaningful. Because I am an outsider, I can approach them with curiosity and few suppositions. Also because I'm an outsider, people don't mind explaining things at the ground level so they're more complete in their explanations and give a bigger picture of how they see their work and the organization.

I begin with inquiry about employees' journeys and meaning models. I have to get beyond work jargon to what matters most. During the interview, I'm learning about the interviewee, but more important, by articulating their story, the interviewee makes connections and awakens to a new understanding of themselves and their relationship to the organization.

Experience helps me listen for things other people might not think to listen for. Some of the pitfalls experience has taught me to watch for:

- People tend to avoid the vulnerable conversation of what is meaningful to them unless there's a catalyst— the birth of a child, a death in the family, or a midlife crisis. So I have to be comfortable talking about meaning in order to empower the interviewee to enter into the dialogue.

- Conversation can meander. Usually, this happens when someone is trying to figure out whether I care enough about the conversation for them to invest in telling me their deeper motives. If I persist with genuine interest, I can usually get to the essential dialogue.

- I avoid coaching specific answers, but that's an easy mistake to make. Once, we held a workshop to teach people how to essence mine and then gave them a chance to mine another person in the group. One participant confessed afterward that while asking his partner about their career choices, he found himself using the interview to "mine" his own fears about his career.

- Sometimes people try to give "safe" answers. They don't use their personal vernaculars at all, but rather parrot what they think is expected. In such cases, I reframe what they said in a way I know won't resonate with them. This compels the interviewee to correct the statement and get really explicit on what they are trying to say.

- During normal conversations, we tend to think analogously. We compare an experience the other person had with one we had; we assume that the words they use mean what we think they mean—even if they're highly symbolic terms. In Essence Mining, that distorts what is being said and damages the efficacy of the process.

Organizational Essence Mining uncovers the structure of the organization's meaning according to its people, so the organization can use this understanding for its journey. It takes more time than individual Essence Mining because there are more interviews, more themes and mantras to parse, and the extra step of bringing the information back to the team for clarity.

It's important to uncover what motivates each individual you're interviewing to join the organization. Then have them articulate, and define, the organization's meaning journey. As you mine 15-20 people, preferably more, you see themes emerge. It is like the eight blind people exploring the elephant. Once, after I had given a talk to a group of healthcare leaders on Essence Mining, one physician left me a copy of this story which relates how each person from their own vantage point, one touching the trunk, one the leg, etc., is expressing their experience. When people haven't familiarized themselves with their own meaning, they often struggle to articulate organizational meaning. But if you get enough accounts of organizational meaning you can tell a pretty detailed story. You're trying to understand what the elephant is from the perspective of each person, then put it together.

The process for Essence Mining the individual is *Mine, Analyze,* and *Synthesize.* This is a lot like the concept of "sharing the picture."

The process for the organization is only one additional step, but that step makes it much more complex:

Mine, Analyze, Synthesize, Personalize.

THE ESSENCE MINING PROCESS FOR ORGANIZATIONS

Mine - The size of the organization dictates how many people Essence Mining will require. With, say, 150 people at one location, I would usually mine 25-30 to get a good handle on the themes and mantras of the organization. I interview people at all levels of the organization—from front line to executives—in various locations.

Some people are better at articulating the meaning of the organization than others, but it's difficult to determine that up front. Sometimes someone who seems introverted has a very precise and detailed understanding of the organizational journey, and individuals who are more vocal are more entrenched in the industry jargon.

Essence Mining interviews typically take 45-50 minutes and begin with Day 1, Breath 1. There are a couple of reasons for this. The most important is that employees didn't make the decision to work at the organization in a vacuum, or even in a process that began when they started their career. Their lives have had a pattern all along, and the choice of where to work, and how much of themselves to put into the job, is part of that pattern. Secondly, people feel a lot more comfortable with the camera if they can begin with their story. It's familiar and comfortable. If you jump into the middle—their career—they have to explain why they are where they are without context. As the conversation and narrative unfold to current day, they reveal recurrences, connections, and behavior patterns.

Any particularly vivid memories they share are probably the ones they're running the most in their minds. As philosopher and psychologist William James said, in his book *The Principles of Psychology*:

> *"My experience is what I agree to attend to. Only those things which I notice shape my mind."*

I ask about these experiences up to the present moment and the current job. Then I ask about the organization:

> *When did you first become aware of this organization?*
>
> *What were your initial impressions?*
>
> *When you were interviewing, was there anything surprising? Any moments you knew this was the right place?*
>
> *What were the elements that drove you to decide to work here?*
>
> *What keeps you here?*
>
> *How has the organization evolved since you've been here?*
>
> *What do you think the organization is doing that is meaningful in society? Meaningful for its customers? Meaningful to you?*
>
> *How would you describe your journey here?*

These are just a few of the questions. We are looking for the individual's meaning language about the organization and how that journey fits their journey.

It's important to listen. Don't ponder the next question. Instead, allow questions to arise that might provide a deeper understanding. Sometimes it's easier for interviewees to communicate through an analogy rather than direct analysis of their experience. This dialogue can't feel like an interrogation; it must feel natural. You can go off script to follow an insight. By keeping the interaction natural and staying curious, I build trust and limbic resonance. My job is to solve the puzzle of the person in front of me.

As they talk, patterns emerge. I reflect those patterns back to the employee to ascertain whether I have a clear understanding. This can also jar their memories about other aspects of the pattern that they want to share.

> *It seems like X has always been important to you. Why is that? How have you tried to manifest that here?*

I pay specific attention to the language to understand their identification with words that communicate significant, meaningful ideas: *What do you mean when you say this word? What is the significance of that idea to you?*

I examine what the person is saying within the business environment. How do they see the organizational meaning as something they can commit to stewarding beyond personal inconveniences? How does the organization provide a conduit for their fulfillment? Where do they have a misperception about what something is, or a defeating narrative? How does that person's narrative align with, or diverge from, the way the organization works?

To find the truth of what the organization is about, I push beyond protective mechanisms such as using business jargon— the language people believe they're supposed to use—and Pollyannaesque enthusiasm. I'm looking for truthful, balanced interpretations of the kind of personal meaning that ignites people's action.

Analyze - Once we have all the videos, we take them back to the lab and watch them, listening for keywords and shared themes. We analyze the mantras that seem to be talking about the same theme across many people in the organization and look for patterns. What have we learned about the people in the organization and how can we connect it to "who" we believe the organization is and how it operates?

Synthesize - Then we begin to synthesize the information into several themes. The mantras, or personal beliefs, that feed into a theme like collaboration might include:

- *I should have the freedom to call anyone in the company to begin a new project if it pushes the company forward.*
- *Ideas should be expressed, then whittled down and collectively agreed upon.*
- *Before launching into a project, you should determine which person is best suited to which task and then let them do their thing. Then everyone can comment when they bring the project together.*

So in an organization where many people say they value collaboration, we have to find out specifically what that means to each person, why it's important, and how it plays out. If an organization just says, "Great! Our employees believe in collaboration" and assigns a meaning to the word that excludes what employees find important about it, they've just created disengagement. Instead, we ask people about the mantras that comprise their core idea of collaboration. What stories do they have in their minds about it? What aspects of collaboration are key to them? Then the team can incorporate those into how they function, so that each person instantly sees their contribution to the way the organization works, rather than merely accepting a static cultural model that may not inspire them. They're also more likely to accept and engage in the parts of the process that aren't their favorite, simply because their needs were also met.

At the end of this process, we have several deliverables, but the most important is a *"vocabulary of rituals and symbols"* that make up the *House of Meaning*—a unique language that defines the meaning of the organization and describes what employees find meaningful. We call it the *organizational lingua franca*.

Today, *lingua franca* means a language that is agreed on by people who speak different vernaculars so that they can cooperate over some objective such as trade, science, or diplomacy. For example, people from different countries might agree to negotiate in English because they all speak it, though it isn't their native tongue. But in the 1500s, *lingua franca* meant a hybrid of many languages used primarily among merchants to trade in the Mediterranean. They were not all forced to speak one person's language, which would have given that trader greater power and status. Instead, they created a language from all their vernaculars.

An *organizational lingua franca* is similar. It's created from the meaning models and expressions of the people who work there, who are defining the meaning journey of the organization. It's an *organizational lingua franca* that defines and exposes the elements that are core to who the organization is. From there, you can begin making the connections between the organization and the people who work there.

Personalize - Finally, you roll out the results in teams and discuss how they connect to the organization. I used to do this with my own teams, asking them to stand up in a group meeting and share what those themes meant to them, whether they resonated with them, and how. We would interrogate specific terms to find out what everyone meant by them. This meaning language is large enough to include everyone's articulations so everyone can connect to it personally.

Once people start understanding how their themes tie into those of their coworkers and the organization, it instantly transforms their perceptions about how they can contribute, as well as how their jobs fit into the larger narratives of their lives. It begins to unveil how they can exercise their individual potentials in this context, which they may not have seen before.

A PRACTICAL LOOK AT ESSENCE MINING

Essence Mining may be unpleasant and painful in the short term but vital in the long term. Sometimes it reveals things you don't necessarily want to hear, but those things are good for the organization. When you mine, it will become clear to you, and your employees, that some people actually would be better off someplace else. Other people think they are in the wrong place because of House Confusion. People can be serving their meaning models, but their frustration with pay or advancement impels them to quit, because they haven't separated those issues into different buckets. Sometimes just separating the houses can begin to unravel long-standing problems.

This is why meaning needs to be stewarded as a separate function within the business, because it has different rules and motivators. It has a different language. No organization would try to run an HR department with the rules of the supply chain. It just doesn't work. Meaning—on its own—is crucial to performance, engagement, and culture. When it gets muddied with the other houses, costly errors can happen.

I have Essence Mined companies where the overarching themes were things like *"Family first," "I have my time back," "Interdisciplinary collaboration allows us to be an organization of firsts,"* and *"People can grow here."* Each had many subthemes and mantras, and each represented the unique personality of the organization. Every time I present the findings to an organization they're delighted and inspired. But in order to be a living company, they must continually steward that meaning.

AFTER ESSENCE MINING
Essence Mining is only the beginning. It gives the organization an authentic foundation to launch a process for meaning. But because the nature of meaning is dynamic, the conversation has to continue and evolve. One thing we experience over and over is that Essence Mining creates a period of elation and connection in a company, sort of like a motivational retreat. But it's a poor investment of time and money if it only generates a temporary high. For Essence Mining to be effective, organizations have to create systems to mine the organization on an ongoing basis and use what they learn to create continuous growth in individuals and the organization itself. That process has to include the vernaculars and meaning of incoming employees as well as those who already work there.

The *organizational lingua franca* needs to be dynamic.

Listening Experience: **Magnification - Yes**

CHAPTER 9

LIVING LANGUAGE

Nobody, not one person, can be a human being by himself or herself. We are tribal creatures. We have to be with each other. —**Susan Schaller**

In 1991, Susan Schaller, an interpreter for the deaf, published a book called *A Man Without Words* about her experiences with a man she called Ildefonso. Ildefonso had been deaf from birth. He knew no spoken language, no written language, no sign. Schaller met him in a reading class for the deaf, and she could see that he was terrified. He watched his classmates sign to one another and mimicked their gestures, but he clearly didn't know what the gestures meant. He kept looking at her as if to say, "Is this right?"

Without language, he had no way to connect with others. He was isolated. When she finally managed to teach him that the gestures of sign represented shared ideas, and that he could use them to communicate with others, he sobbed.

Ildefonso's story is an extreme one. But it mirrors how people function in a culture where they can't meaningfully interact with those around them. If you don't actually connect with what's happening, your only option is to parrot what others around you are doing and saying and hope to create a connection. You're not communicating anything real about yourself, only that you, too, can share in these messages and behaviors, constantly questioning: "Am I doing it right?"

ALL THAT IS SAID; ALL THAT ISN'T

By and large, social interaction is governed by unconscious rules. Extroverts are given more attention than introverts. In most meetings, leaders do 80 percent of the talking, says Lindred Greer, an organizational behavior professor at the Stanford Graduate School of Business. In the 20 percent of time remaining, much of it is spent agreeing with the leader, and often only those who have deeper voices or are perceived by the group as more attractive or powerful will garner the group's attention.[31]

Greer thought these patterns might be evolutionary. But there's more involved. Most people—especially those who are not yet individuated—learn early on who has power, whose favor to curry, what to reveal, what to conceal, whom to support to bolster their status. They know all about Procrustes' bed.

So a discussion that's supposed to be about how to exceed customer expectations, or how to employ user experience to tweak the product line, is a dance of status, power, and popularity that hinders organizational objectives and potential. No organization deliberately creates this; it's natural group dynamics. But as Greer pointed out, it leaves many people with no voice. The assumption is that if they don't speak, they have nothing to contribute. Too often they adopt that assumption as well, and wind up filling a perfunctory role as a disengaged employee.

Just inviting people to contribute doesn't work. Most of us know our place in the pecking order. The higher you get to the top, the more protective people are of what is said—and how it is said. Because of all the careful "couching," leaders often develop the mindset that people need to approach them in a particular way, which renders the conversation parental and constricts honest, authentic communication.

Having a process for organizational meaning helps transform the culture by clarifying the dialogue. No longer are people dumping personal baggage on the leader, repeating the group chant or asking "Is this right?" Instead, they're all finding their way out of the cave, together. Employees may never before have contemplated the question:

"What do I believe matters most to the organization, and is there any connection between that and the tasks I do every day?"

When you ask these questions, employees are more likely to look for meaning in their work. This calls people out of seeking authority-based meaning and into the beginning stages of curating their own meaning. Instead of shrinking back and only offering what seems to be asked of them, they have to look at their roles, their contributions, their motivations. It's the beginning of individuation, or self-authoring. The roles that we have in life and in our organizations are not imbued with purpose or steeped in meaning. The roles are transformed, and transformational, because we make them so. The role serves the organization when we accept full responsibility to imbue it with meaning, not hoping the next role might provide it.

When our meaning is satisfied, we're content to focus on exploring the full potential of our role and ourselves within that role. In turn, that role in the organization is transformed and we are transformed by it.

And, more importantly, the organization is transformed in the process.

BRINGING THE ORGANIZATION TO LIFE: ODLF

The word is protective magic against the daimons of the unending, which tear at your soul and want to scatter you to the winds. You are saved if you can say at last: that is that and only that. You speak the magic word, and the limitless is finally banished. Because of that men seek and make words.[32] —**Carl Jung**

Words can make something finite by defining it. By the same token, symbolic words can have infinite meanings. Words can both create a fence around an idea, and can simultaneously expand our understanding of a given idea. The way we use language either shrinks or enlarges us.

But let's face it: If you had to have a lengthy discussion about meaning and vernaculars every time you tried to accomplish something, nothing would ever get done.

Essence Mining is a core process for uncovering the organizational House of Meaning. It takes the responsibility of our need for meaning off of the leaders—who can't possibly be expected to fulfill it—and puts it squarely on the shoulders of the individual, where it belongs. It liberates the other houses from having to explain or carry meaning. It identifies the shared meaning that helps employees understand why they might be in the right place and how they can serve their meaning, and the organization's, at the same time.

Building the organizational lingua franca gives you a shared language that everyone is responsible for. It can—like the languages of the first three houses—speed things up and enable efficient communication so people can work together effectively.

But you can't stop there. The organization is on a journey, so the meaning, and the meaning language must evolve. It has to be dynamic as the human community is dynamic. A living company needs an organizational dynamic lingua franca that can transform not only the organization, but the individuals within it.

When everyone has a role in articulating organizational meaning, they're more likely to feel empowered and committed to serve their own meaning models and potentials through their work. The meaning is their baby now. They own it because they helped draft and shape the language that defines it. While they were doing so they were listening, working to understand and make connections between their articulations and their coworkers'. So because everyone was open, listening, and crafting the language together, they now have a more expansive and profound comprehension of the organizational meaning and the people with whom they work. I've often heard one employee say of another's articulation: "I really like what George said about the way we collaborate. I never thought of it that way before, but it's true." In that process, their understanding about the organization is growing. The language and their understanding of the meaning evolve in the process of the dialogue.

When you use an ODLF, you avoid soundbites that could apply to any number of organizations. You're looking for individual vernaculars, for everyone's meaning of the words, so you can identify your organization's unique—and probably more complex —meaning. "Customer experience" could mean myriad things to different people, so it's important to understand what that looks like and what it entails for each person. It could be that someone will articulate the idea in a way that resonates with everyone. But there's also the risk that the "popular" person's vernacular may win more support from the group than that of a less popular participant and be adopted as a Stage 2 authoritarian meaning system. That's why it's as important to seek out unique perspectives as it is to identify the obvious. People asked to communicate something authentic from their core know not to fall back on "groupthink." Because they're asked to, everyone becomes a little more comfortable with expressing the most essential parts of themselves. They can be more truthful about how they see things and feel about something.

Sharing your truth around meaning, out loud, in a group of people doing the same, is empowering. It reinforces a sense of unique identity and serves as a platform for further efforts at individuation. Having everyone in the room, regardless of social aptitude or position, working to understand your vernacular and how it aligns with their meaning contributes to belonging and redraws connections according to something deeper than standard power dynamics. Such a scenario discourages the kind of silos that create division, because individuals are rewarded for their uniqueness, rather than the power of their alliances. For many people, just starting this conversation and building a system of meaning together launches, or progresses, their journey of individuation and self-actualization. Until they do so, the organization cannot self-actualize.

This is totally different from individualism—every person for themselves. It's a shift in perspective from "What do I get?" to "How do I serve this organization on its journey?"

"How can my unique talents help contribute to offering new possibilities for the collective benefit?"

During Essence Mining conversations, team members often recognize a shared mantra that unites them in limbic resonance in a way they might never have otherwise known. Sometimes when two people suddenly discover they have one connection point—like when Bijoy and I began talking about the book *The Self-Aware Universe*—then multiple connection points appear. Two team members who might not have known they could fulfill their potentials better by collaboration often discover that they can. And they begin to recognize and appreciate the uniqueness of the other in that collaboration. This is essential in multi-generational, multi-cultural workforces.

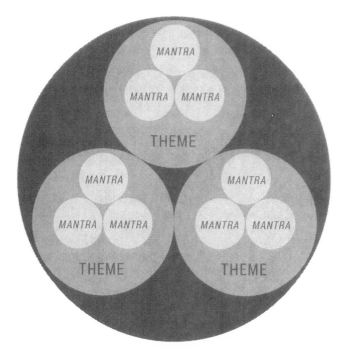

ORGANIZATIONAL DYNAMIC LINGUA FRANCA

In building the ODLF, you both fence in the meaning language to something that everyone can use, a shorthand that helps work get done faster and more efficiently, and you leave a gate open for future refinement. This is the way to build a human community, not through enforced cultural enthusiasm but through invitation for the whole human to contribute. This transforms a static company into a living company.

HOW CULTURE WORKS

The Roman philosopher Cicero coined the word culture. His definition was "to cultivate the soul." Today we've forgotten Cicero's definition and think of culture as a noun for the collective rules and rituals of a group. An organizational culture tends to be a fixed thing, but that's not so with societal cultures. The Economist Intelligence Unit, researching global engagement, pointed out that corporate culture is expected to be swallowed, almost like a pill, while the societal cultures from which people emerge develop slowly and become part of a person's identity.[33] Getting many people to swallow the pill doesn't impact their identity or what they have to offer an organization, nor does having everyone swallow it together create cohesion.

Cultures, by nature, are not static. Each new generation brings change. Social, economic, and environmental circumstances force change. And with these changes, ideas and behaviors are created, recycled, and repurposed. The culture must be an expression of those who live in it and must evolve as they evolve. And just as with social cultures, the language of an organizational culture must evolve as well. The ODLF you begin with will not be the same six months or a year down the road because the people who created it will be evolving and new people will have joined. Together these employees will discover the current ODLF's limitations and find better articulations. The new articulations will help to transform everyone's perceptions and thoughts about themselves, the organization, and their ability to serve the customers. Once you take the lid off growth and feed it, it's self-perpetuating. As the process for stewarding meaning evolves, the individuals—or at least those who aren't resistant to change—will also evolve, and the understanding they have of themselves, their contributions, their coworkers, and the organization itself will continue to expand and deepen.

INNOVATION IS EVOLUTION

The effect of this is known as cultural ratcheting. Cultural anthropologists believe that culture is cumulative. Each step forward is shared by the whole group, and thus each person's contribution raises the entire culture. This is where innovation comes from.

Sociologist Joseph Henrich has done copious research on the nature and origins of innovation. In most cases, he says, innovation does not come from one person interacting with the environment. It comes from numerous individuals building on one another's unique approaches to a problem or a question. From an initial articulation, each new person contributes their unique twist, pushing the idea forward. Henrich calls this social learning. He points out that having a lot of minds working on a problem is the difference between innovation and stagnation. He has written about how populations that shrank suddenly also lost their ability to innovate. Tasmania was on the same technological trajectory as Australia until the Bass Strait flooded 10,000 years ago, separating them and reversing Tasmania's ability to innovate.

But proximity isn't all that's required. Henrich said people are naturally disinclined to share their ideas. Instead, they learn as much as possible from others without exposing what they know. They are more likely to share, he said, if there is considerable interconnectedness and they believe it's for the good of the group. Interconnectedness comes from sharing themes and mantras and from having a safe space to articulate your meaning, in your vernacular.

It contributes to performance, too. An international group of researchers discovered that in higher-performing teams:

- More teammates contributed to the communication than in lower-performing teams.

- Team members' interconnectedness revealed itself through the use of emotional language.

- When someone's language became less emotional and personal, it was a sure indicator that this team member was getting ready to leave the organization.[34]

In other words, innovation and performance happen when team members feel emotionally connected to one another and encouraged to contribute to group communication. That's what an ODLF provides.

Once it becomes a normal part of the conversation, the ODLF weaves itself into all of the conversations about operations. Many conversations in business intertwine the houses of phenomena, rights, resources, and meaning. The discussion about how to tackle a project or work with a new client, for example, might include elements of all of these. But when the objective is discussed using the shared ODLF, reflecting what's meaningful to the people who will be doing the work, the conversation is elevated to a level not previously reached. There's a qualitative difference between talking about increasing sales as a goal of the house of resources versus an aspiration of realizing shared meaning.

Essence Mining and the ODLF are tools for becoming a Stage 3 organization. It's the process for self-actualization, individuation, self-authorship, at scale. It's not pushing levers, hoping to hit the meaning one, it's infusing personal meaning and responsibility into the veins of the organization and creating a mechanism to keep the blood flowing.

And that has implications for humanity.

Listening Experience: **Mr. Blue Sky - ELO**

CHAPTER 10

HIGH FIDELITY

High Fidelity was a film about a music-obsessed guy who, after getting dumped by another girlfriend, sets out to see what has gone wrong in his relationships by revisiting old girlfriends. In the process, Rob (played by John Cusack) learns that in most cases he and his girlfriends never really understood each other. And he never really committed to the relationships, even though he thought he had. The movie is an excellent metaphor for what is happening in today's organizations. We often talk past each other, never really resonating, never having the essential conversations. So we never establish real trust or fidelity—something both organizations and employees ultimately want.

This book has explored a new approach for establishing that trust and fidelity through creating those essential conversations using the process of Essence Mining and the ODLF. We have explored new lenses with JOurneY and Human Fugue, which help us examine what is truly meaningful to the organization and the individual. These are tools that create a deeper understanding of the relationships we have in business and life—empowering us to experience the resonance of a higher fidelity.

In trying to unlock a hidden code that would help organizations find and hire highly skilled professionals, I stumbled onto a solution for the engagement problem for organizations. Looking back it makes sense. Recruitment had to be the canary in the coal mine. Engagement starts with the first encounter. Having an essential dialogue about what matters most paves the way for easier integration into the organization. The new employee naturally goes to work acclimated with the right intentions. Or they quickly realize there is not a fit and everyone can make more expedient decisions to move on.

But it couldn't work if we only understood the candidate, because the glimpses we had into the organization revealed so little of what it was like to work there every day. Occasionally, we'd have a person cycle back through the recruiting process, and, when we asked why they'd left the organization, it was because of things we couldn't see from the recruiting standpoint.

Organizational leaders haven't had the tools to deal with the real complexities of how disparate people work, communicate, and connect. As de Geus said, "Because the workplace was full of people, it looked suspiciously as if companies were not always rational, calculable and controllable." Without tools to deal with that fact, leaders are at a loss.

Harvard professor David Perkins did research showing that 90 percent of the errors in thinking aren't because of faulty logic, but because of faulty perception. If our perceptions are wrong, the thinking that follows will be off-track too. A critical step is to clarify perceptions—within the individual about their journey, among coworkers about their shared meaning, and around "who" the organization is, why it exists, and how each person can contribute to that specifically through their work. This ongoing essential dialogue permeates every other conversation that happens in the organization.

Even during the early phases of the Essence Mining interview, people's perspectives shift. Something clicks. Just changing the conversation to how everyone in the organization can fulfill their potentials—become more fully themselves as they work— makes people more open and curious about the meaning in their work. And they're more likely to re-examine what contribution they've actually been making through their respective roles. My friend David Beaver, director of the Cognitive Science Program at The University of Texas at Austin, said that the very act of engaging someone in this type of dialogue changes the way they think about their company and their job. On a cognitive level, the process of examining the organizational meaning begins the process of evolving it.

In my journey of understanding organizational essence, I talked to Dr. BJ Fogg of the Stanford Persuasive Technology Lab. What he said stuck with me: "You are working on a really interesting problem—the problem of helping people to make high-impact decisions." That makes sense, because decisions that affect our lives and the things that matter to us must first be touched by the limbic brain with all its connection to emotion, memory, and symbol. Decisions are high-impact because they're meaningful.

Meaning has always been a key factor in high-impact decisions, but it hasn't been recognized as such. We had no system for it, so we tried to operate as if it wasn't there. We've been pulling meaning "levers" when we're trying to motivate someone, make a decision, or sell to a customer. But meaning isn't a lever; it's more like DNA. It's a part of the system that's often overlooked because it's been poorly understood. Management scholar Edward Deming pointed out that when organizations and societies lack a system, they tend to see incidents as isolated, often looking for someone to blame for a bad result. They tend to miss system-wide issues that, when resolved, can improve system-wide results. Until now, meaning has been confused and baked into the other systems.

Our clients have used Essence Mining and the ODLF to design recruiting process communications and management approaches. But it could be a powerful tool to help create cultural cohesion among diverse groups or ease the cultural tensions that often precede merger and acquisition failures. It took two decades to develop these tools, which were well ahead of the trends. Art Markman, director of the University of Texas' Human Dimensions for Organizations master's program, said: "It takes a lifetime to effectively diagnose and solve very hard problems in business, but once the tools are there they can be taught to a lot of people very quickly."

The Essence Mining mindset is one of inquiry and integration. You discover what is there and integrate the information into existing systems, rather than trying to make the world line up to a narrow set of expectations and beliefs. It requires suspending judgment, clarifying and putting language around elements of a situation in which there's cognitive dissonance. Using these tools to understand meaning builds pillars of trust.

The possibilities keep unfolding. Leadership, innovation, marketing, and, of course, recruiting can all benefit from trust.

LEADING THE WHOLE HUMAN

Implementing meaning as a process in the organization does not require leaders to become therapists or counselors. They're not responsible for the emotional lives of their employees. But employees are whole human beings whose limbic brains and unconscious drivers prompt a lot of their actions. These aspects of human functioning can be the chief energies behind commitment, connection, and performance, or they can leak out into workplace drama. It's to the benefit of the leader to channel them into fulfillment of individual potential through the work. If you think of the leader as the Wise Old Man—a Gandalf, Morpheus, or Yoda—none of them spent much time massaging the feelings of their apprentices. But they must provide the environment where people feel both safe and inspired to embark on what is always a somewhat messy process of uncovering and fulfilling their potentials. Growth is always accompanied by mistakes. The mistakes you want to avoid are those of carelessness, sabotage, neglect, or simply not understanding the goal. Essence Mining and the ODLF address all of these.

Organizational and team leaders can conduct conversations around individual meaning tied to the tasks employees must perform, the organization's key performance indicators, and providing value to their customers. Just as a leader might ask, "How much will this cost?" and, "Who is in charge of making decisions?" they can also inquire, "How can you serve your meaning through this?" As these conversations continue, employees take more and more responsibility for serving their meaning models and fulfilling their potentials by fulfilling the potential of the organization. This greatly reduces the burden of management to direct their actions and motivate their performance. When meaning is shared, explicitly, the question becomes: "Did I serve the organization, and myself, to the best of my abilities today?"

Then it becomes the leader's job to "hold the circle" as the whole organization progresses on its journey.

Holding the circle is guitarist Robert Fripp's term. Since 1969, the progressive rock band King Crimson has evolved through a carousel of musicians, different instruments, and different sounds, always connected with musical technology and famous for its democratic approach. Fripp, the only band member who's been part of each incarnation, is the band's de facto leader. He once told members of the band Tool that he felt like it was his job, throughout the various manifestations, to "hold the circle" for King Crimson. He needed to evolve the essence of King Crimson through its many changes. "The aim is not to follow any one person, but to be sensitive to the group as a whole," he told Tom Mulhern in an interview for Guitar Player magazine in 1986.

By making a space for the people in your organization to be who they are and offer what they have to contribute, you become a dream weaver. You weave everyone's passions, and the dreams of what they are capable of, into a vision of getting something done for the company, the customers, the world.

RECRUITING

I've written extensively about how we use essence to recruit. The conversations are immediately deeper and more effective, focused on finding someone who can contribute meaningfully to the organization. We're not driven by time-to-hire, dragging dozens of near-miss candidates into the hiring manager's inbox to prove how busy we are. Nor do we sell opportunities to people who will leave in a year, triggering the whole expensive process all over again. Our work is more fulfilling when we can put people in positions and explore great opportunities for alignment. Using essence to recruit enables us to inspire productive conversations on how someone is best able to contribute.

I have a long-term client, a head of HR at a major Midwestern medical center, who once explained that after they had started using Essence Mining, the right candidates started showing up in her inbox. One powerful Essence Mining video was of a young doctor telling the story of a day that a patient showed up late. It was a particularly busy morning, and the doctor said she didn't have time to see the patient now. Then an older doctor took her aside and said, "You have no idea what it took for that patient to get here. You will see that patient." Anyone who watches that video interview will understand what the medical center is about, my client said, and anyone who's turned off by it isn't someone they want to hire anyway.

When recruiters focus on money—House 3—and skills—House 1—rather than on matching essence, they're commoditizing the process of human interaction. That might be OK if you were buying a commodity, but you're orchestrating relationships. In response to the pressure to solve a temporary problem, hiring someone on a skills-and-money match generates several longer-term problems, such as a diluted culture, dissatisfied employees, and turnover nightmares. Think about the message you send to your employees when you cut corners on a hire: Culture is not that important to us; we say we value relationships, but we don't live what we say. Missing out on the essence match is like having a blood transfusion with the wrong blood type. That may sound a bit dramatic, but disengagement, turnover, and dissatisfaction rates are profoundly dramatic.

NURTURING CREATIVITY

Many studies have shown that the No. 1 factor affecting job satisfaction is autonomy: the freedom to do the work the way you see fit, as long as the results are good. To engender autonomy is essentially the same as building an environment in which people can fulfill their potentials. When you let the employee create a process that works for them, rather than defining the process, you require them to engage their intelligence and creativity. You've moved them from a Stage 2 model to a Stage 3, self-actualizing one.

A lot of organizations seem to have reservations about actually giving employees autonomy. At the same time, they complain of a dearth of creativity. They may have "blue sky" sessions where people are supposed to throw out creative ideas, then go back to their work stations and perform tasks according to a template someone else devised for the sake of efficiency. Creativity doesn't work that way.

According to Edward de Bono, the world's leading authority on creative thinking, people have to be expected to be consistently creative. Creativity can't be flipped on and off like a light. The directive must come from the top. When employees lack autonomy and understand that there are "right" and "wrong" answers, they unconsciously listen for cues to reduce cognitive tension so they can contribute. Their brains select the most relevant details to solve the problem efficiently according to common beliefs or best practices.

But research into creativity shows a much less rigid way of thinking. People focused on a specific goal tend to exhibit gamma and beta brain waves. But in creative mode, or "flow" state, the predominant brain waves are alpha and theta waves. These are the same kind of waves that occur when people are beginning to fall asleep, that period where your brain starts interposing wakeful thoughts with dreamlike thoughts.

Creative people often appear—to those less creatively inclined—unable to focus or drill down to the information set the situation requires. But in fact, a creative person's tendency not to filter information from their surroundings or their imagination is what allows them to synthesize new ideas, according to Scott Barry Kaufman and Carolyn Gregoire, authors of *Wired to*

Create: Unraveling the Mysteries of the Creative Mind.

As neurologist Fredrik Ullen of Karolinska Institute in Stockholm was quoted as saying: "Thinking outside the box might be facilitated by having a somewhat less intact box."

Yes, there are some people who just don't want to think. They don't want to work that hard. They prefer the ease of an authority-based system. For those people, you have to determine whether they're doing all they need to do without serious cognitive connection, or whether they need to go. But the chances are that more of your employees are creative than you know—or than even they know. If it's only their skills and ability to follow a template that are invited into the workplace, then neither of you will ever find out. When you ask how someone can serve their meaning in their work, you open up whole realms of thought people might never have explored in terms of imagination, experience, emotion, and memory. They're able to recall times when they created something they were proud of, when they used their imaginations, and to draw on those resources for the work before them. And once people open up that box of potentials, they tend to keep discovering more. You can't make a person creative. But bringing meaning into the work equation gives power to their autonomous efforts and provides fertile soil for creativity to grow.

MARKETING

Joe Pine has been ahead of the curve on consumer business models for quite some time. In his 1992 book, *Mass Customization*, he pointed out that our economy was becoming customized. He saw this coming a full 16 years before Chris Anderson pointed out that we were in a "Long Tail" economy. In 1999, Pine partnered with James Gilmore to publish *The Experience Economy*, followed by *Authenticity: What Consumers Really Want*. He wrote about consumer markets, which reflect social/psychological shifts that also drive workers' expectations. As reflected in Pine's books, we've become people who want what we want the way we want it. We're not interested in someone selling us a lifestyle or an idea that doesn't mesh with who we are. We don't want to be sold. We want companies to tell us who they are and then let us decide if they're for us.

Look at Dos Equis' ad campaign featuring *The Most Interesting Man in the World*. He's clearly an actualized person: He rearranges the art in art galleries, he aces a Rorschach test, and people hang on his every word. Yet he isn't saying, "To be like me, you have to drink Dos Equis." He makes a very personal statement: "I don't always drink beer (clearly an understanding and respect for consumer preference). But when I do, I prefer Dos Equis." When imported beer sales dropped overall at the launch of this campaign, Dos Equis had double-digit increases.[35]

Customers are looking for an experience. Your employees are responsible for creating that experience. Which means you'd better make sure they experience the organization in a way that you want them to project out into the world.

Southwest Airlines, which has always focused on customer experience, specifically hires with one item on the top of its list: empathy. In interviews, candidates come in as a group and take turns standing at the front of the room sharing their most embarrassing moments. Then employees watch the faces of the seated candidates, looking to see which ones demonstrate empathy. Those are the ones it pursues.

Yes, the airline puts a heart on its planes, but it also enables employees to express themselves uniquely as part of the brand.

CHECKING IN

Human-centric marketing and customer experience that's responsive to individuals rather than classes of customers, that engages people authentically with empathy, can only be created by people who are expected to bring their humanity to work. It has to be OK to be aspirational, goofy, intense, or idiosyncratic, so long as you channel it into having empathy for the very human customers you serve. Essence Mining and building an ODLF expand everyone's empathy and understanding of the many ways employees and customers might see the organization. The meaning conversations that build interconnectedness among employees can also be used to create a bond with customers. After all, they're on a meaning journey, too.

START WHERE YOU ARE

Of course, it's ideal when Essence Mining and an ODLF are developed across the organization. But individual teams can do this, too. They can do Essence Mining and create their team or departmental dynamic lingua franca according to how that part of the organization functions. They can identify how the top performers' meaning models and language contribute to their performance. They can map the tasks they must accomplish to the Human Fugue. They can have group meetings about how employees see their meaning models being served in their day-to-day tasks, or how they don't. They can examine what avenues there are for growth within each person's meaning model. They can map out their meaning journey.

Each area of an organization is different. The work requires different actions and different skills, and this shapes a different language. Sometimes it's hard for people to see how their meaning models contribute to the organization overall. Once, a chief of staff at a hospital I essence mined took the people from the finance department through a hospital to see how resources contributed to patient care—how the various suppliers of the medicines and medical equipment delivered tools to help doctors, nurses, and other healthcare providers do a better job. He explained why some tools were used over others. Before this tour, this division was completely removed from the day-to-day interaction with patients, which was the meaning of the organization. This chief of staff gave the members of the finance team a connection with what the organization was really about.

AT PLAY

Remember when you were a kid, and you took on a project where you worked hard, maybe got sweaty and tired, and focused so intensely that when someone called you to dinner, you looked up, shocked? You might have collected small cuts and bruises, wrecked your clothes, forgotten to eat lunch. But all you felt was the exhilaration of bringing your idea to fruition. And while you were deeply engaged, time disappeared.

We never really stop wanting to play. But meaningless play isn't fulfilling. (That's why video games go out of their way to involve people emotionally in the illusion that there are stakes.) There's nothing more exhilarating than tapping your creativity, pushing your limits, learning and growing in the pursuit of doing something that matters. As Maslow said, work is play for self-actualizing people. It is its own reward. Some of the characteristics of an organization that empowers play include:

Emphasizing learning and curiosity over knowing. The most creative people are those who are open to new experiences. Your team needs to look for new experiences rather than replicating the same successes.

Tapping the collective intelligence. The more minds that work on a problem—and the more disciplines, perspective, observations, and imagination they bring—the more innovative and creative the solution will be. If everyone is standing at the elephant's trunk, no one will ever understand the elephant.

Fostering true empathy. Employees need to begin with compassion for themselves, acceptance that they are human, and that humans have both things we're not proud of and potentials they haven't even begun to tap. Next, they need to understand that everyone else—their bosses, their coworkers, and their customers—are likewise human and likewise hungry for the feeling of being truly alive. They need to ask themselves how everyone—employees and customers—can make this journey toward fulfillment of potential and a meaningful life together. How can they continue to grow?

We've reached a place where many people can't find meaning in institutions and don't know how to find it in themselves. We've forgotten that the organizational journey is always a human journey. Markets don't change because of numbers, they change because people change—in their habits, their appetites—usually in response to very human motivators like fear, growth, and curiosity. But without developing competencies for meaning, we're hobbled from dealing with that truth. Human language, meaning language, taps that place where the whole person is engaged. That's where dreaming, imagination, and creativity come from. That's when we focus not on the answers, but on the possibilities; we connect with sales numbers, and with what our customers want and need as people. The language we use, and feel encouraged to use, tells us which part of "us" is invited to the conversation—the bundle of skills with the ready information, or the human being with empathy and imagination?

Children at play are often engaged in the imaginative process of the work ritual: the lemonade stand, the role of mommy, the role of soldier. They are immersed in the creation of a work world while they play. They identify the significance of the "work" they're doing with what that role means to them. As we move into the world of work, many often leave that symbolic, immersive part behind, just as we leave the language of human expression behind. But that's where genuinely unique ideas spring from.

Consider the smartphone, the driverless car, biophilic design—all ideas that started with imagination and "What if?" Many of our breakthroughs or even iterative innovations happen when someone cares enough to break the brittle pattern of common thought.

When we examine our meaning, we change our motives. When we change our motives it changes how we act. This changes how we think. We have spent a lifetime speaking things into existence. So when we begin breaking down our meaning models to examine what resonates and what doesn't, when we begin to question the validity of the presuppositions in our models and rewrite the code, we can initiate a veritable cascade of new awareness.

We are in the midst of a monumental shift that will surpass what happened in the industrial revolution. Increasing amounts of research and effort are being made to help this shift occur. Welcome to the beginning of the revolution to tap the potential of the whole human.

We are engaged in this every day. We invite you to engage with us.

ACKNOWLEDGEMENTS

I would like to express my gratitude to the many people, who saw me through this book. I am not shy in seeking out challenging conversations or advice. I cannot thank enough those who stayed in the conversation with me, read a rough draft I called "beta," offered comments, allowed me to participate in their organizations or Essence Mine them.:

Melissa, Rachel, Colton.

Bijoy Goswami's contribution to this book is immeasurable. The models, conversations, insights, challenges, support, and commitment. A driving force in the materialization of this book.

Susan Lahey for holding the line on keeping the prose smooth while working through very topics with multiple layers.

Jay Long for friendship, energy and putting these models to work with honest vigor.

David Payne for the commitment to pushing the envelope with me on a lifelong learning journey.

David Beaver whose conversations and interest in Essence

Mining always shine a perspective on these topics.

Art Markman: "It takes a lifetime to diagnose and solve very hard problems, but once the tools are there they can be taught to a lot of people very quickly."

Philip Vanhoutte for evangelizing Essence Mining, Meaning models and your commitment to helping polish what needs to be polished.

Terence Bennell for his after-hours efforts, precision aesthetic and detail in the formatting and production.

I would like to give a heartfelt thank you to the following people that engaged with me on the "Beta" copy of the book, Essence Mining or furthering the cause:

Hugh Downs, Greg Baker, Steve Golab, Ashland Viscosi, Boyd Stephens, Wendy Gores, Jonathan McCoy, Amanda Zhu, Bo Durickovic, Eric Saperston, Sarah Maren, Jen Freitas, Fred Schmidt, Jim Bullard, Tim Hamilton, Katie Bailey, Ruth Yeoman, Michael Griffin, Pat Poels, Lynne Peterson, Walker Houghton, Clay Spinuzzi, Pam Holloway, Heath Rezabek, Neeraj Bansal, Ronan Cosme, Pam Bennison, Jennifer Reidy, Kim Pritchard, Max Borders, Mihran Aroian, Karen Aroian, Asha Cooper, Jennifer Horvath, Lisa DeMoss, Daniel Messick, JP Taxman, Kyle Thomas, Guy Carr, Kathy Weir, Ashley Allen, Tera Eng, AZSHRM.

I would also like to thank the following authors and artists for contributions to my thinking:

Carl Jung, Abraham Maslow, Peter Drucker, Susanne K. Langer, Joseph Campbell, Paul Kugler, Michael Porter,

Mark Granovetter, Barry Schwartz, Edward L. Deci, Marcus Buckingham, Arie de Geus, Mihály Csíkszentmihályi, Noam Chomsky, Peter Senge, Douglas R. Hofstadter, Matthew E. May, Edward de Bono, Steven Pinker, Arthur De Vries, Robert A. Johnson, David Bohm, Charles Darwin, Robert Sapolsky, Geoffrey A. Moore, Hermann Hesse, Johann Wolfgang von Goethe, Edward T. Hall, Joseph Henrich, James Hollis, Charles Taylor, Allen Wheelis, David Whyte, D.T. Suzuki, Erich Neumann, Friedrich Nietzsche, Marie-Louise von Franz, James Hillman, Robert Greene, Joseph Chilton Pearce, Otto Rank, Salvador Dalí, Maynard James Keenan, Rush, Tool, Yes, Sting.

For more information on suggested reading, and links to models in this book, visit:

essencemining.com

REFERENCES

CHAPTER 1

1. C.G. Jung, *The Undiscovered Self* (New York, NY: New American Library, 1958), 17.

2. Michael Porter, *Competitive Advantage: Creating and Sustaining Superior Performance*, (New York, NY: The Free Press, 1985).

CHAPTER 2

3. "State of the American Workplace," *Gallup Inc.*, <www.gallup.com/reports/199961/state-american-workplace-report-2017.aspx>, (March 1, 2017).

4. Susan Sorenson and Keri Garman, "How to Tackle U.S. Employees' Stagnating Engagement," *Gallup Inc.*, June 11, 2013, <www.gallup.com/businessjournal/162953/tackle-employees-stagnating-engagement.aspx>, (April 4, 2017).

5. William A. Kahn, "Psychological Conditions of Personal Engagement and Disengagement at Work," *Academy of Management Journal* 33, 4 (Dec 1990): 694.

6. Abraham Maslow, "Theory Z," <www.maslow.org/sub/theoryz.php>, (March 1, 2017).

7. Maslow, "Theory Z."

CHAPTER 3

8. "The Interview Process," *Harvard Business School*, <www.library.hbs.edu/hc/hawthorne/07.html>, (March 1, 2017).

9. Alex Edmans, "The Link Between Job Satisfaction and Firm Value, With Implications for Corporate Social Responsibility," *Academy of Management*, <http://amp.aom.org/content/26/4/1.abstract, September 2, 2012>, (April 4, 2017).

10. Teresa Amabile and Steven J. Kramer, "The Power of Small Wins," *Harvard Business Review*, May 2011, <hbr.org/2011/05/the-power-of-small-wins>, (April 4, 2017).

CHAPTER 4

11. Amabile and Kramer, "The Power of Small Wins."

12. Whole Foods Market, "Declaration of Interdependence," <www.wholefoodsmarket.com/mission-values/core-values/declaration-interdependence>, (March 6, 2017)

13. Brad Tuttle, "The 5 Big Mistakes That Led to Ron Johnson's Ouster at JC Penney," *Time Inc.*, April 9, 2013.

14. Dan Ariely et al, "Large Stakes and Big Mistakes", (Boston, MA: Federal Reserve Bank of Boston, 2005), <www.bostonfed.org/economic/wp/wp2005/wp0511.pdf>, (March 1, 2017).

15. Edward T. Hall, *Beyond Culture*, (Garden City, NY: Anchor Press, 1976), 218-9.

16. Steve Jobs, "Steve Jobs' Vision of the World," <www.huffingtonpost.com/2011/12/01/steve-jobs-vision-of-the-world_n_1123782.html>, (April 4, 2017).

CHAPTER 5

17. Barbara L. Fredrickson et al, "A Functional Genomic Perspective on Human Well Being," *Proceedings of the National Academy of Sciences*, July 2, 2013, <www.pnas.org/content/110/33/13684.full>, (March 1, 2017).

18. David Eagleman, *Incognito: the Secret Lives of the Brain*, (New York, NY: Pantheon, 2011), 1.

19. Andrew Newberg, "How Our Brains are Wired for Belief," *Pew Research Center*, May 5, 2008, <www.pewforum.org/2008/05/05/how-our-brains-are-wired-for-belief/>, (March 6, 2017).

20. Robert J. Hoss, "Recent Neurological Studies Supportive of Jung's Theories on Dreaming," *R. Hoss*, 2012, <dreamscience.org/articles/Jung_and_Neuroscience_Hoss_2012.pdf>, (March 1, 2017).

21. Abraham H. Maslow, *The Farther Reaches of Human Nature*, (New York, NY: Penguin, 1993), 78.

CHAPTER 6

22. Milton Friedman, "The Social Responsibility of Business is to Increase its Profits," New York Times, September 13, 1970, <query.nytimes.com/mem/archive-free/pdf?res=9E05E0DA153CE531A15750C1A96F9C946190D6CF>, (March 1, 2017).

23. Arie de Geus and Peter M. Senge, *The Living Company: Habits for Survival in a Turbulent Business Environment*, (Boston, MA: Harvard, 2002).

24. Rev. Don Cupitt, "Inheritance of Dreams," Carl Jung, The Wisdom of the Dream, Vol 2, <www.youtube.com/watch?v=CQUsUMVd8XM>, (March 6, 2017).

25. Duff McDonald, *The Firm: The Story of McKinsey and Its Secret Influence on American Business*, (New York, NY: Simon & Schuster Paperbacks, 2014), 15.

26. Ceridwyn King and Debra Grace, "Internal Branding: Exploring the Employee's Perspective," Journal of Brand Management, December 7, 2007, <www.palgrave-journals.com/bm/journal/v15/n5/full/2550136a.html>, (March 1, 2017).

27. Arie de Geus, *The Living Company*.

28. David Whyte, "The Conversational Nature of Reality," <www.onbeing.org/programs/david-whyte-the-conversational-nature-of-reality/>, (March 1, 2017).

29. Alessandro Duranti, *Linguistic Anthropology*, (New York, NY: Cambridge University Press, 1997), 8.

CHAPTER 8

30. Ken Blanchard, "Collaboration - Affect/Possibility," TEDx Talks, TEDxSanDiego, <www.youtube.com/watch?v=HKGkBRk1kSo>, (March 1, 2017).

CHAPTER 9

31. Ross Kelly, "A Stanford Professor Identifies the Top 3 Problems with Top-Down Leadership," Chief Executive Magazine, <chiefexecutive.net/stanford-professor-identifies-top-three-problems-top-leadership/>, (March 4, 2017).

32. C. G. Jung, *The Red Book = Liber Novus, A Reader's Edition*, (New York, NY: Norton, 2012), 250.

33. Economist Intelligence Unit, "Engaging and Integrating a Global Workforce," <futurehrtrends.eiu.com/report-2015/executive-summary/>, (March 1, 2017).

34. Peter A. Gloor, "What Email Reveals About Your Organization," MIT Sloan Management Review, November 2015, <sloanreview.mit.edu/article/what-email-reveals-about-your-organization/>, (March 1, 2017).

CHAPTER 10

35. Jeremy Mullman, "Dos Equis 'Most Interesting Man' Is An Even Greater Beer Salesman," Ad Age, July 15, 2009, <adage.com/article/news/dos-equis-interesting-man-a-great-beer-salesman/137963/>, (March 1, 2017).

CPSIA information can be obtained
at www.ICGtesting.com
Printed in the USA
FFOW03n1425060218
44943689-45196FF